Happy Birthday Carol!

May this "new year" bring you closer to your PASSION and inspire more magic and joy into your life!

Best Wishes,

Gina Matijs xo.

Aug 2015

DYNAMO DIARIES

DYNAMO DIARIES

V1

*Success Secrets
of 21 Shining Stars!*

Compiled & Introduction by:
James Erdt

LIVING WELL & DOING GOOD

Copyright © 2015 DYNAMO Publishing
All rights reserved.

Compiled & Introduction by: James Erdt

Printed by Next Century.
Available from Amazon.com, DYNAMOentrepreneur.com, JamesErdt.com and other retail outlets.

This book may not be reproduced in whole or in part, in any form or by any means, electronic or mechanical, including photocopying, recording or by any infomation storage and retrieval system now known or hereafter invented, without written permission from the publisher.

DYNAMO Publishing & Creatives Director is Tracey McLeod.
Cover design and layout by DYNAMO Creatives.
James Erdt, Chief Architect of WOW Photo, by DQC Photography.
All background graphic images © GraphicStock.com.
All chapters and images are copyright of the authors.
DYNAMO Publishing & DYNAMO Creatives are divisions of DYNAMO Entrepreneur *(DYNAMOentrepreneur.com)*

ISBN-13: 978-1514279199 (CreateSpace-Assigned)
ISBN-10: 1514279193

WELCOME to the *DYNAMO Diaries!* This project is specifically designed to inspire you to BE THE BEST VERSION OF YOU by learning through the success of others.

I am your host, James Erdt, the Chief Architect of WOW for DYNAMO Entrepreneur, a company that focuses on social entrepreneurs who are "Living Well & Doing Good" around the world. The Team DYNAMO is absolutely thrilled to share the first group of 21 uber-talented co-authors in DYNAMO Diaries Volume 1 with you. This compilation is part of an epic series of seven books showcasing nuggets of wisdom that have made each writer successful throughout their life's journey.

A true DYNAMO Entrepreneur's vision of health, wealth and life-balance in this modern information age should be about EVEN MORE free time and EVEN MORE mobility to enjoy mini-retirements and extended vacations, while living life to the fullest versus saving all the gold necessary for the illusion of a safe retirement later in life, with a very unpredictable and unsecured future.

Life is meant to be lived NOW. By investing in things such as your body, mind, spirit and well-being PLUS precious memories with family/friends and relationship capital, you will be much happier, more fulfilled and authentically abundant. True success is an ongoing journey; it is not a destination far away in the unwritten future. Lasting happiness is a choice. Your choice. Here and now.

This book will act as an oxygen mask; it will revive you and inspire you to live a healthy, active life of walking the talk so you can feel alive—and thrive. Regardless of the decisions you made or what happened to you in the past, you can turn your life around in light speed simply by making a choice to do so. Start today. Get over your own negativity; stop playing the blame game, the victim role and that horrible disease known as *"excusitist."* The only person you truly have control over is yourself. Be the change!

This book will support you to take charge of those passion projects you've always wanted to do. It will help you to correct your course along the way instead of never ever getting started and living a life of regret. You can create your dream vision board of achievement and truly see what it feels like to be, to do and have the life you've always dreamed of.

Focus on good and smart balanced choices in the moment, making one proper decision after the next with positive reinforcement and affirmative action, in order to live life with confidence as you move towards your goals. Get ready to get uncomfortable and push past the limits you have imposed upon yourself. That's how you grow. That's how you evolve. That's how you thrive!

The DYNAMO Diaries co-authors will share tips, tricks and their success secrets so you too can positively experience the best life has to offer. They'll teach you about self-reliance, as we all need to remember that it's not about the resources you have, it's about how resourceful you are. These authors support your understanding regarding results and effectiveness. They will help you to work smarter versus working harder and sometimes moving in the wrong direction. They will guide you to live in abundance versus scarcity. Each author thoroughly enjoys supporting others, bringing them great satisfaction and fulfillment knowing that they are giving back to others—which is what life is all about.

We are the DYNAMO Tribe and our DYNAMO Diaries are dedicated to you, our valued reader. Enjoy!

Discover / Develop / Deliver,

James Erdt

Chief Architect of WOW

DYNAMO Entrepreneur

NOTE: *To discover and learn more about the multiple DYNAMO Divisions that support business professionals and small business owners across the board with leading edge products, exceptional services and empowering events, please visit DYNAMOentrepreneur.com and sign up for the mailing list to stay up to speed with everything DYNAMO. Also see and contribute online to #DYNAMOtribe.*

Table of Contents

The 4th Secret 13
By Ash Silva

Finding My Voice, Writing My Story, Living My Vision 21
By Amber Scotchburn

It Begins With You. And Living Your D.R.E.A.M. © 29
By Andrea Ivanka

Relationships, Relationships, Relationships 39
By Bonnie Chan

My Three L.U.V Principles – Recipe for Success in Life and Love 49
By Carmelia Ray

Defining Success: Live Life on Your Terms 57
By Crystal-Marie Sealy

The Road to Success is Not Always Paved 67
By Dana Janzen

When You Almost Die, You Wake Up 75
By Fahad Buchh

Forbes Riley's Remedy: Overcome to $uccess 83
By Forbes Riley

Have a Little Faith 91
By Gillian Faith

If You're Looking for a Sign, This is it! 99
By Gina Hatzis

Wake the Flipper Up
The Simple Formula To Unlocking Your Purpose 107
By Giuditta Gareri

Spiritual Warrior 115
By Ilina Ivana AstroCoach

Pure Success 123
By James MacNeil

People First, Before Anything 129
By Jey Jeyakanthan

The Illusion of Self-Worth 135
By Jordan Ovejas aka Mr. Magic

Finding You... a Dance of Courage Back Home to your
Authentic Beauty 141
By Josephine Auciello

Miracles Do Happen 149
By Kamil C. Kowalski

Laura Bilotta's Three Nuggets of Wisdom 161
By Laura Bilotta

Your Life is Your Gift 167
By Sara Notenboom

Find Your Passion and Keep Tremendously Interested in It—
From a Health Coach Who's Been There 173
By Susana Andres Mignosa

DYNAMO DIARIES

The 4th Secret

By Ash Silva

Sipping on my Turkish coffee one morning, I contemplated my recent success. As I basked in the sunshine I was warmed with gratitude and appreciation for the amazing, incredible life I have. I began to wonder what the success formula was that has earned me the very life I enjoy today.

In my pursuit of success, I first had to ask myself, what is it that I am trying to define and what does success really mean to me? The answer was as clear as listening to Earl Nightingale himself say, "Success is the progressive realization of a worthy goal or ideal." The end goal that is important to me is to leave people I encounter included, appreciated and respected. This goal, which is the basis of all my work, has truly helped me consistently gain and materialize success.

As I continued to sip my coffee, the three most important factors that have contributed to my success became clear. They glared at me boldly yet beautifully, even glowingly. I took another sip in honor of my realization.

1. Celebrate People

One of the greatest lessons I learned while growing up, in wanting to connect with others, to be accepted into the group, to be picked for teams and to contribute to the common vision, was the art and science of celebrating others. What does it mean to celebrate others, beyond the birthday party?

Growing up in Bombay, India and coming to Canada to settle in Toronto at the tender age of eleven, I don't remember much celebration. The only celebratory occasions I was involved in as a teenager were various parties and consumptions. There were, in fact, lots of gloomy times with no celebration—in school, at home, and in between.

Celebration is the simple art of acknowledging yourself, honoring others and revelling in the world around you. It comes from a place deep within us that transcends conscious thought and behavior. I believe we all have it within us, waiting to be discovered—like a long lost secret or treasure. I remember realizing my sense of celebrating was gone; in fact, I wondered if I ever really had it, like many people around us today. Yet, once discovered, celebration can take on a celebration itself.

I don't believe that I am alone in my want to be loved and cared for, even admired and acknowledged, understood and respected. Think about the people you meet and what they want from you in that very first meeting. What do your friends want from you? What value to the relationship do you bring?

I uncovered the secret as my career in the corporate world of sales took off. The common denominator I found among the super successful achievers was their ability to celebrate, respect, understand, honor, listen, and even admire everyone around them. From friend to foe, acquaintance to prospect, client to the chance encounter that left you touched and wondering if you'd ever meet again, people were moved and inspired just because you were who you were in that moment.

The art and science of celebrating people is the most overlooked and the least understood, yet the simplest and most profound way to influence people and win friends you ever want to learn. When done with authenticity and transparency, celebrating the other is the most potent leverage to instantly engage anyone. This all begins with initially engaging someone where they first like you, then know you and trust you enough so you can earn their business.

Exercise to Discover the First Secret to Success:

1. What is the best example of someone celebrating another person that you have witnessed in your life so far or that you know of?

2. What is the ultimate example of how you can celebrate someone *today*?

2. Create Win-Win Situations

The best deals are the ones where everyone feels they got the best and most benefit working with you.

Before I even dare engage with a potential client to ask for business, whether it is giving a quote, preparing a proposal, or asking a question, I first explore how all the parties can benefit from what I am thinking of offering to them. I further explore what the best possible outcomes can be so that everyone wins by engaging in the relationship.

The stronger the sentiment from each party that they got the better end of the deal, the more strategic is your win-win plan. Where the first secret was active in its celebration, creating and implementing win-win scenarios is where the "rubber hits the road." This is the action step that realizes and materializes success as I have experienced in my own life.

We have all come across the people who operate on the other end of this spectrum. These are people who are takers as opposed to givers, who have selfish motives instead of selfless ideals, who want to use instead of contribute to a common vision. People who cannot see past their own ambition, wants, needs, and desires, and who will sometimes stop at nothing to get what they want at the expense of those around them. Success, achieved through selfish means whether short lived or not, is not fulfilling or satisfactory.

The pleasure of success, I believe, lies in the act of contribution. Yes, sometimes that can mean to give and give more without getting in return, but it also means creating win-win solutions that actually leverage much more business, volume, and wealth because of the alignment than the two parties would have accomplished separately.

Exercise to Discover the Second Secret to Success:

1. What is the simplest win-win suggestion you can think of in any realm of your life? Suggest it today!
2. What is the most strategic win-win idea or strategy you can think of that will leave all parties inspired to do business with you *today*? Make that call *now*!

3. Your Fortune is in Your Follow up—Consistency is Key

How many times have you witnessed the best intentions going nowhere? Lots of celebrating people only to wake up the next day and "celebrate" elsewhere. Or even moving from active to action by sending quotes or creating those unique win-win scenarios only to do the same again and again.

We can spend a lifetime attending networking events, lunches, seminars, and tradeshows; meeting people and collecting business cards as we celebrate those people in the moment and then create win-win scenarios to entice all parties to come together and take action. The biggest secret and possibly the hardest one to keep on an on-going basis, is the third secret of success. It is where everything happens. It is where the money is made, wealth is created and legacy is left. Nothing happens until what began as a celebration of someone becomes a win-win idea, proposal or deal for both parties to celebrate each other's victory by celebrating their own. The key lies in the follow-up and the consistency and quality of the follow-up.

Consistent follow-up serves at least two purposes:

a) It brings in more business—period! Whether you subscribe to the stats that say most sales are made after the seventh engagement, or you just see and smell it from experience, consistency is the key to cash flow. Of course, a system to automate the follow-up to keep it consistent is the final "piece de resistance" where you can begin to systemize your success auto-magically.

b) It brands you as a serious player, running a serious business that you take seriously. The reason most sales are made after at least a few interactions is because this is how long it takes for people to get to like you, know you, and trust you. Only then does this success formula that consists of the three secrets shared so far—the celebration of others, creating win-win strategies, and consistent follow-up—create the success I enjoy today.

So by watering, nourishing, and combining these three secrets to success over the years, I enjoy reaping the rewards of my cultivation by not just harvesting more business, but by actually enjoying the hidden fruits of my toil.

Exercises to Discover the Third Secret to Success:

1. Think about three people who you may have celebrated with and would like to celebrate with again, and who you want to do business with—and then *follow-up*.

2. Search for some online tools and calendars that you feel would help you automate your follow-up and implement only one tool today.

   As I emerged from my day dream, still basking in the light of contemplation, I noticed time had stood still for me to have had all those realizations that flashed through my life, summoning the most coveted secrets I earned. But just as I realized that time had also past in a flash as my coffee was still hot, the fresh aroma awoke me to new possibilities.

I took a deep breath of the fresh morning air and couldn't help but become only too aware of how these three secrets to success have really helped me—beyond business—beyond the many friends and acquaintances—and beyond the obvious. It came to me…

…the 4th secret…

I took another sip and drank in the appreciation of an amazing life. Though something told me, this was only the beginning.

Ash Silva

Ash Silva is an author, speaker, connector and entrepreneur.

Born in Bombay, India and coming to Canada at age eleven, Ash enjoys the diversity and philosophy of the east and west and brings that experience into his business and his personal life.

When not committed to his full-time passion for business, networking, and connecting businesses to resources, opportunity, strategies, and more business, Ash loves to spend as much time as possible with his five beautiful children.

Connect with Ash at http://AshSilva.com

Finding My Voice, Writing My Story, Living My Vision

By Amber Scotchburn

My name is Amber and I lived in an abusive relationship. I am sharing this as a fact, just as I would tell you what I had for dinner. This is my journey of how I separated myself from my story.

My transformational process began with what I have coined my "wake-up episode" on December 16, 2008. It was on this day that I reached out for help and acknowledged to myself and to a team of professionals that I was in an abusive relationship. The snowy storm outside was akin to the storm inside my home. This "wake-up episode" transformed my life; it brought me to my present conscious state—a place where I feel happy "just because" and I feel a richness beyond wealth.

During my transition, there were mornings I would wake and for a couple precious seconds I would forget what was happening in my life. Then when it hit me, it was like a stab to the heart. These were days when I had to carefully select my thoughts just as I might select my clothes for an important event. It was a new habit to learn and a very powerful one at that!

If you have ever played the "what if" game with yourself, you can understand all the complex thoughts and processes that were roaring through my brain. I've since realized that the "what if" game is not productive to things that are in your past or your future, because all you have is now.

I sought answers as to why I stayed in an abusive relationship. Why did someone (me), who had studied the abuse cycle in school and who had the training of a professional, stay locked in such a situation? I would like to mention that I have a social work degree and have over twelve years of mentoring and working with "at-risk" populations. In my head I really thought I should have been immune to this. Sadly, few are not touched by abuse.

What I learned was that every behavior has a need associated with it. I was getting something out of the relationship or I would not have stayed. In coming to this understanding, I learned that my predominant strengths of being a loving, compassionate, nice human being were being continually fed— even though these same strengths were at risk!

You see, I love to love. I thought my love would overcome anything. I started my career in social work and quickly realized that I wanted to take everybody home with me to care for them. I knew this was not conducive to being in that profession, so I used the extraordinary communication skills I had learned and together with my passion for people I switched careers. I earned my teaching certification and flourished in creating dynamic programs for the "at-risk" populations in the school system, and contributed to amazing success stories.

I thought that the theory I applied to my professional role, which was that all someone needs is one person in their life to show them unconditional love to help them transform, applied to my personal life, as well. I do not want to say I thought I could change the person but I want to suggest that I thought it was possible for him to heal because of my love. Ironically, this type of relationship fed into my own need for love.

I was empathetic to my partner to the point of being detrimental to myself. When working with at-risk populations, being able to truly put yourself in their shoes and see what the world could look like from their perspective is powerful. This strength enabled me to create the successful programs that I did. However, transferring this empathy to an abusive partner was done at my own expense. I was more aware of his feelings than my own and I catered to his feelings above mine. Our greatest strength can also be our greatest weakness; an excruciatingly hard lesson to learn.

Here is the thing; I was brought up to be "the nice girl." This meant that I did what I was told, what was expected of me, and what was deemed right. I rarely spoke my mind in issues related to me. I held my thoughts in, even though it was slowly killing me inside. I was scared of not being perceived as the nice girl; I never wanted to upset anyone. In essence, I was taught that it was my fault if someone treated me badly and it was selfish to put my needs first. I was the perfect partner for someone who was abusive.

In being a loving, compassionate, nice human being, I suffered greatly in that I lost the deeper understanding of who I was and what I wanted in life. I was stripped of my house, my furniture, my partner, my job, my life savings, and my world as I knew it while simultaneously moving five provinces. I had two adorable children and I needed to support us. My overwhelming circumstances could have been a cause for a breakdown—instead I had a breakthrough.

Living on Vancouver Island in British Columbia Canada (if you don't know where that is, you should Google it) is like living within the most picturesque movie set you have ever seen. Finding a professional job is difficult because a lot of professionals want to live in such an ideal setting. This meant that even with a Bachelor of Social Work, a Bachelor of Education, and over twelve years of fantastical work experience, the jobs I could secure would pay the bills but not fulfill my life. I will never forget sitting in what was my third interview, for a job totally unrelated to my education or career experiences, and having the job offer in front of me to sign. This job would have meant a pay cheque every two weeks with a cubicle of my very own, one and a half weeks of vacation a year, and maybe two hours a day with my kids.

Being stripped of everything that defined me could not be reconciled by a cozy cubicle and a secure pay cheque. So how could I break through to be true to myself?

I started my own business, Amber Scotchburn Training Consultants, which is a life skills-based training company. Our company motto is "Advancing Knowledge, Transforming Lives." I started two training programs simultaneously: *Learn to F.L.Y. (First Love Yourself)* and *Tutoring...With A Twist*. Both programs were born out of a need to earn money doing what I loved to do and what came most natural to me. That is, believing in somebody when they didn't believe in themselves and re-engaging somebody in life, all while building a relationship of trust with them and myself. Both programs were started out of my living room and have flourished into recognizable programs in our community!

The *Learn to F.L.Y. (First Love Yourself)* program was born when I felt as though I could not possibly go on. I had to channel my inner child and remember that from their stand point, anything was possible. By helping myself transform, I am now able to give people the means to help themselves through having their own "tool box of life." If they need to "fix" something that isn't feeling quite right, they can go to their toolbox and see what will help them adjust themselves. This might look like meditation for someone, an exercise video for another person, a phone call to reach out to someone they love, a journal to record their thoughts, a vision board to glance at, an online group to share with—and the list goes on.

Tutoring...With A Twist was initiated as I realized that not everybody taught or learned the way I did. I believe in teaching and assessing students in multiple ways to address all the different learning styles that exist in a classroom. And beyond that, teaching students how they learn so they have the language and tools to use to be more independent learners and thinkers. This means training students to solve their own problems by being able to find their own solutions. Don't you wish you had this when you were growing up? I place academic skills and life skills on the same plane of importance, so we work with someone on their math skills while we simultaneously teach them how to use an agenda. We believe in working as a team and that means many inclusions in a child's life such as their parents, teacher, coaches, mentors, counsellors—it really does take a village.

I am who I am. I am not defined by who I was, who I wanted to be, or who I thought I should be. Part of my past has brought me to my today and that is it. Sometimes you may need to indulge in something that has happened to you and give yourself permission to experience whatever is coming up. And then you need to move on from it. The transformation in people who have felt the kind of release that happens when one moves on from a story they are stuck in, is mind-blowing.

I risked a safe, meaningless existence to create opportunities for myself and come out whole on the other side. I could let go of the the guilt of feeling as though I didn't have enough love to heal my partner. I could let go of the guilt of not giving my children the storybook perfect life. I could be a statistic and still be proud and happy! I could want love and family and seek healthy ways to find them. I could speak and be valued. I could start fresh from that realization moment and go forward and just be me.

I am truly happy, feel blessed, and am in awe with what I "have." I am meant to be where I am and I am thankful every day for the wealth that I do have. I practice being grateful for my life every moment. Having a deep gratitude for where you are in life at any given moment allows the universe to open up endless possibilities, whereas having a "poor me" mindset is limiting and non-productive. By shifting to being happy "just because," I am not waiting for something in my life to happen or for completion of a whole check list of things to find happiness. I get to decide. I challenge you to be happy "just because."

When I was going through this transformation, I had a blank artist canvas that I used to illustrate a point. The blank canvas had the foam word "believe" in front of it. This was to symbolize that sometimes we are not going to know the path we have to take or have the answer immediately to a question or problem we need to solve. However, having faith that the universe—simply because we have acknowledged the problem and stated that we were looking for some guidance in that area—will help in figuring out a solution. Imagine co-starring with the universe in the movie of your live and you have to trust your co-star!

I get to do what I love every day, which is to help people. I have created a company based on my skill sets and the needs I see in society. I am building a company in which people see the value in what I am creating. It is a journey of its own, re-shaping and transforming within itself, and I continue to learn about this entrepreneurial journey. This is truly amazing. And guess who ultimately transformed through my love, compassion, and niceness? Me!

This is my journey: it is a journey of how I became aware of what was important to me in life and the path I took to find success to define my values and beliefs and offer them forward. It is a journey of awareness that has led me to the understanding that life is actually pretty simple in that we create our lives by the choices we make. I am making my life a masterpiece; how about you?

Amber Scotchburn

Amber Scotchburn is the founder of *Amber Scotchburn Training Consultants*, a life skills based training company. Amber's training programs are an interactive process of teaching and learning. They enable learners to acquire knowledge and develop attitudes and skills, which support the adoption of healthy behaviors.

Amber's diverse educational background, including a Bachelor of Social Work and Bachelor of Education, is fused with her passion for people and has empowered her to be a dedicated leader in developing innovative curriculum and teaching methodology. Combined with Amber's energy, enthusiasm, and initiative, this has resulted in a solid commitment to build trust-based relationships throughout communities and implement leading-edge educational and training programs.

Tutoring...With A Twist is one of the most successful educational and training programs Amber has designed. It is a full-service tutoring agency located on Vancouver Island and is looking to expand to a city near you.

Amber lives with her family on Vancouver Island. She is passionate about life-long learning, living her life to its fullest, spending as much time as possible outdoors, staying connected to family and friends, and savoring really good food.

www.amberscotchburn.com
www.tutoringwithatwist.ca

It Begins With You. And Living Your D.R.E.A.M.©

By Andrea Ivanka

> *"I have a dream."*
> **Martin Luther King**

Inside all of us is a dream, a vision, an idea of how we want to experience life. No matter what age you are or where you come from—it begins inside of you—a dream that whispers of how it might be. Maybe you've already heard it calling.

Hi! I'm Andrea Ivanka, the communication catalyst and creative brains over at Andrea Ivanka International. Some might tell you that I'm also the instigator of innovation, and fan of making learning and transformation fun. For those of you who don't know me yet, I'm an explorer, world traveller, and avid reader.

Let me share something with you, something that's been in the works and building for almost fifteen years now. It's what I believe to be the basis of innovation and a huge breakthrough so that you can step into your life with passion, authentic connection, and transformation. I call it the Live Your D.R.E.A.M. Blueprint©, and it's come out of all the experiences I've had in my life—the good, the bad, and the downright ugly—with all the nuggets of wisdom pulled together. Now I want to share them with you.

Before we go on, let me tell you a little bit about myself.

For the past fifteen years, I've travelled, taught, and worked all over the world. From Canada to Mexico, to China, to the U.K. and back, everywhere that I've lived I've had the privilege of serving in leadership roles and found myself speaking, creating curriculum, running training programs, and getting people clear out of their comfort zone. I've done everything from running international meet-up groups, to handing out food and hammering roofs on humanitarian aid trips.

As I travelled, what really started to fascinate me were the people I met who were shaking up the status quo. The people who didn't quite fit in "the box"; the dreamers, the catalysts, the change agents. The people like me, who imagined a new way of doing things and then found a way to make it happen. What's super exciting is that I see more and more entrepreneurs and leaders doing the same thing: embracing the need for trust, connection and value, and carrying it out into the world.

This chapter is dedicated to all of you who are on the journey of authentic service, transformation and empowerment.

Now all that's great, but can I be honest for a moment?

I have to admit that I used to really struggle with this whole idea of "just being myself." Who knew?

Before I realized how awesome my vision and my dream was, I used to lose myself trying to prove to the world that I was *just* like everyone else. I thought that I had to continually prove myself so that I could "fit in" and "be accepted."

No matter what I did, sail across the English Channel and back on a 42-foot Bavaria; live in Mexico for three years; work in both the UK and China, deep inside I felt as if my "outside the box" way of living meant that I just didn't fit anywhere. (For story details, visit www.andreaivanka.com)

I believed that my ideas for how the world "could be" didn't have value because they were different. Everywhere I went I wanted to show people that they were amazing, creative, and capable of just about anything instead of the typical "you did this wrong" way that they'd been taught to operate and motivate from. At the time, I truly believed that I'd never really be able to have a career doing what I loved because I thought my ideas were too different for anyone to understand. Sound familiar?

I felt as if I was living inside a huge pressure cooker. The authentic me would come out—but only when it felt safe. It was a weird place to be in, sometimes myself and sometimes not. It was impossible to completely hide myself because at the heart of it, I was passionate about learning—and truth be told, somewhat of a nerd. A world travelling, outgoing introvert (figure that one out), but a bit different, nonetheless. And because I associated "smart, outside the box, creative" with "not fitting in" whenever I created something new with massive results, the compliments would slide right off me. Craziness, right?

And here's the kicker, I subconsciously created barriers along my pathway to success so that I could "prove" that I was different and that I didn't fit in. I got to be right. The look on my face when I finally figured that one out!

On the surface, it looked as if I had it all: travel, a great career, and great experiences. But slowly, this pressure to fit in took the joy of the adventure, the passion, and the fun right out of my life. It was the perfect recipe for disaster and when it hit, it hit hard. I experienced the kind of trauma that I'd never wish on any woman—with after-shocks that affected me on many levels.

When I finally snapped out of denial, I knew I had to get real. In the process, I chose to focus on many of the positive moments in my life; that doors *had* opened for me all over the world; that people *really* liked me; and that I *had* incredibly innovative ideas on how to shift education, learning, and business training to be fun. And more important than all of those, I realized that one incident, no matter how terrible the moment, should never define a person. *I refused to become a victim of my own story.*

I realized then that I needed to let go of my need to prove my worth and fit in all the time. I had to *decide to be myself*—and hold true to my vision wherever I was in life. In the process, I went on a journey that brought me to where I am today—a board certified trainer in four areas and owner of a Board Approved Training Institute. I'm also the CEO of a growing company dedicated to helping entrepreneurs and leaders infuse their lives and their careers with passion, connection, and power communication. Why? So they can step into their power, own their voice, and live the dream— *authentically!*

Look around you; we're seeing it everywhere.

Innovation, authentic communication and being of service are **more important today than they have ever been before.** All over the world people are starving for acknowledgement, craving connection, and looking at how they can be the best possible version of themselves. I believe that we need to light a match of breakthrough and fan the flame of empowered leadership—worldwide.

It begins with a D.R.E.A.M. Yours. So, let me share with you what the ***Live Your D.R.E.A.M. Blueprint©*** is and how focusing on these simple steps will bring you to success—each and every time. (I should add here that I was supposed to give you three nuggets of wisdom; you're getting five because that's how powerful the ***Live Your D.R.E.A.M. Blueprint©*** is.) Let's begin!

1. D – Decide, Distinguish and Drive

   Tool #1: This is the first step and it's key to moving forward. You need to get real on what's going on in your life, in your business, in your world. Decide what needs to be done, distinguish what's holding you back—where are you most challenged—and dig down deep to find the inner drive to take the next steps. This is the beginning of response-ability. Everything begins with *choice* and until you've decided, nothing happens.

2. R – Release, Relinquish and Restore

   Tool #2: At this stage, it's about cleaning up the past, releasing limiting beliefs, negative emotions, and the limited stories about who you are. This is about changing the negative self-talk that's going on in your head. Let's face it, whether you're in business for yourself or working within an organization, wherever you go, *there you are!* So if you're carrying around mind-numbing gunk from the past, it's going to stop you flat in your tracks—outside of your awareness.

   To accomplish this, I use the most powerful release tools on the planet from boardroom to battlefield—Creating Your Future Techniques ™. Going through this process literally transformed my life and the *best* part was that I didn't have to share details about my "stuff." Sweet relief let me tell you! Once you're released you can relinquish that knuckle-gripping control you used to have on every little detail of how it was "supposed" to be. Restoring is about using NLP and tapping you back into all the internal resources and skills that you already have, and that make you totally awesome, capable, and ready to take on the world.

3. E – Educate, Enhance and Empower

   Tool #3: Alright, so now you know what you want, you've cleared up what's been holding you back and tapped back into your inner powerful you. That means that you're ready to bridge the skills gap. Educate thyself. It just makes sense that when you're out making your goals a reality you're going to need to learn a thing or two, doesn't it? Things like how to connect with others so that they instantly feel safe and validated; how to get into peak states in seconds; and most importantly, how to be yourself while communicating more effectively so that others "get" your vision and climb on board—it's called captivating your audience. To find out how visit www.andreaivanka.com. You might want to try and build an isolated bubble—I dare you! Then laugh along with me when "you get stuck"...Success happens in relation to others, in community.

   Once you've got all that learning down, you're in a sweet spot to enhance your skills, your vision, and your message. Then it becomes easy to tweak along the way so that you're living from an empowered state—and creating that ripple out into the world.

4. A – ACTION, Accountability and Audience

    Tool #4: "A" is the feel good results in reality space. It's where rubber meets the road and you're taking daily *action* steps to get you toward your result. This is where you start to build in accountability pieces such as joining a mastermind to keep you on track. This is also the growth period of taking your message out into the world and sharing it with others whether it's through speaking, webinars, or in small intimate groups. It's one of my favorite steps and it's truly where the joy of the adventure starts to bubble over. And it's *mandatory* (yes, it's a must) that you celebrate your accomplishments here! All of them. Why? Simple: to program yourself for success.

5. M – Master, Motivate and Mentor

    Tool #5: CONGRATULATIONS! Your journey has brought you to unconscious competence (find out what that means on my blog) and you're now able to get creative with what you've learned. Welcome to the mastery stage. This is where inner-motivation shines through. Best of all, because you've hit the success that you wanted—all while being authentically you—the doors to show others *how* they can do it, too, are open. You're able to mentor and pay it forward.

There you have it. The **Live Your D.R.E.A.M. Blueprint©** is a guaranteed step-by-step method that you can use over and over for success.

Now that you've had a taste of what it means to really D.R.E.A.M., you're probably wondering, "What's next?" I'm grateful you asked! Considering that for some of you, this is only the beginning of your journey and you'll need to know exactly what to do after you *decide* to move forward, I'm going to give you one simple step. Visit www.andreaivanka.com and get connected.

You see, I believe that *everyone* deserves to follow their own unique path. There's so much more I'd love to share with you so you can stop hiding and finally discover the authentic self that's ready to become the next-generation leader in your field, no matter what that field is. Refuse to look back in a year and say, "I wish I had..." Go discover what's possible so that you can begin putting a powerful plan of action together "NOW."

Until next time!

Andrea Ivanka

An author and established speaker, Andrea comes from a background that has always included educating and empowering aspiring leaders. Over her career, she has spoken to over 7,000 people worldwide.

As the CEO of Andrea Ivanka International, Andrea divides her time between developing live accelerated learning courses for the busy professional, programs for individual clients, interactive training events, and connecting with members of the local communities of the west GTA.

Andrea is the creator of Influence Like A Pro, and Captivate Your Audience – two NLP based professional programs designed to help service professionals and entrepreneurs have breakthrough results while getting more clients through clarity, confidence and power communication. The programs assist clients in identifying what has been holding them back so that the step powerfully into success, make more money and have fun along the way.

The results speak for themselves: Individuals and companies move forward with powerful momentum, high personal participation and increased innovation while achieving massive results.

Andrea loves travelling by train, adores Mexican food, and can say "Thank-you" in at least eight different languages. Her guilty pleasure: books.

Feel free to drop by and say hello on Facebook https://www.facebook.com/AndreaIvankaTrainer or via Twitter @AndreaIvanka

She'd love to hear from you!

Relationships, Relationships, Relationships.

By Bonnie Chan

"What do you want to be when you grow up?"

If you ask a child this question, you'll at least usually get a pretty cool answer like, "I wanna be a race car driver" or "I want to be a princess."

If you ask a teenager this question, you'll get more answers like, "I want to work for company X" or "Maybe this, maybe that."

Then, if you ask a full grown adult this question, you'll hear a lot of, "I have no clue, but I know that I don't want to work for anyone anymore."

I think there is an entrepreneur in everyone, but like a baby, the creative self needs support and guidance to flourish.

When I was eleven, I started my first job babysitting, and my first business inspiration was to have a team of babysitters working with me. I even went so far as to draw up a promotional poster, but I never showed it to anyone. I had the dream, but the entrepreneur inside me wasn't ready to come out yet.

However, just a few years later, in high school, the entrepreneur inside me started to bud. I had a part-time job assisting with the adult night school. One day I noticed that there was nowhere for the night school adult students to get food and snacks. I spoke with our principal and got approval to set up a stand selling cookies and chips to the adults during their class breaks. That was my first taste of entrepreneurship and I wanted more...

In university, my boyfriend Aaron had a passion for photography and loved spending money on cameras and equipment. Since he was investing all this money on his gear anyway and loved taking photos, I convinced him to start a wedding photography business. He was a good photographer, but the entrepreneur inside him was buried deep down, so it was up to me to get this business rolling. I reached out to all of my friends to ask if anyone knew of couples getting married who wanted a free secondary photographer for their wedding. Also, at these weddings I made sure to connect with the professional photographers—one of whom became our good friend and took Aaron under his wing. He became a mentor to Aaron and many years later would be the photographer at our wedding. In no time, we built a solid portfolio, raving fans, and a steady stream of referrals. We even landed a wedding gig in Malaysia.

Although I didn't realize it at the time, Aaron was my first client and business success story. I was able to combine his photography skills with my network and relationships to create a solid business.

> *"Give a man a fish and you feed him for a day. Teach a man to fish and you feed him for a lifetime."*
> —Chinese Proverb

Today, I've come to realize that my true passion is not just connecting people to my network, but rather, it is to inspire and empower entrepreneurs to network for themselves and to give them the tools they need to nurture and grow relationships that will take their business to the next level.

Three philosophies that I live by and that have served me well in my entrepreneurial journey:

1. Build and cultivate relationships.

I believe that this skillset is the key foundation for success. I have dedicated the last decade to study, teach, and master this skillset.

Looking at all the jobs I've ever had from the part-time ones while I was going to school to the corporate jobs after I completed university, 90 per cent of them were found through my networking efforts. My business successes from wedding photography to currently training and coaching all started with, and continue on, through word-of-mouth marketing.

You see, many people leave their corporate jobs and start their own businesses. Why are so many of them successful right away? It is because they already have established relationships with customers and vendors, industry partners, manufacturers, and suppliers.

Relationships aren't just beneficial for career and business. They are for everything in life.

For instance, on my first wedding anniversary I wanted to do something special, but I didn't want to spend a lot of money. I knew someone who knew someone who owned a $6 million, 14,000 square foot mansion in the Vancouver area, and I knew that most of the year it was vacant. A few phone calls and days later, we landed the spot and had a most spectacular mansion anniversary vision board party in exchange for a donation to the charity that the owner supported. The home was absolutely immaculate and because our wedding anniversary is on December 29, the mansion was still decorated with lights, Christmas trees and holiday cheer. We had over fifty friends and family members spread throughout the huge living and dining area of the mansion, cutting out photos of their goals and dreams from magazines and pasting them on Bristol boards—

There aren't many places in the world that we want to go to where we don't have a friend(s) or at least a friend of a friend. In a recent trip to Chicago for a weekend seminar, we had one day off and connected with one of my past coaching clients who took us on an amazing personal tour of the city and a live concert at Millennium Park in downtown Chicago. In a few days we are heading to Costa Rica and I am certain we will meet up with friends and local connections there.

Of course, just as we need to exercise and keep our muscles strong, so must we continue to cultivate our relationships. The worst thing you can do is call up someone out of the blue and ask for a favor or try to sell them something after you haven't spoken in years.

People who know me call me the Master Networker, not just because I meet and connect with people wherever I go, but because I take the time and effort to cultivate and grow these relationships daily.

> *"You can have everything in life you want, if you will just help enough other people get what they want."*
> —ZigZiglar

ZigZiglar said it best, and his quote really is the cornerstone trait of a master networker.

My mom and dad are great examples of this. When I was growing up, they helped people who were in need, with no expectations, just because they had been there and they knew how tough things could be. In my opinion, my mother is one of the most resourceful people in Vancouver.

Some of my favorite personal habits are picking up the phone to sing "Happy Birthday" to someone on their birthday; smiling at everyone, especially the grumpy looking ones on the subway ride; playing the contribution game and asking people in my life how I can help them; and sending unexpected heart-felt greeting cards and gifts.

2. Be grateful and expect good things to happen.

> *"Be thankful for what you have; you'll end up having more. If you concentrate on what you don't have, you will never, ever have enough"*
> —Oprah Winfrey

In our household we have a family ritual that started when my first son was two years old. We call it the gratitude circle and every night, either during dinner or before bed, we take turns sharing what we are grateful for that day. One of my son's favorite lines is, "I am thankful for thankfuls."

I am grateful that "Thank You" is one of the first phrases I learned in language.

I am grateful for wonderful friends and family.

I am grateful and happy for the abundance of events available offline and online.

I am grateful to meet interesting people every day.

I am grateful to live in a country of freedom.

When I attend any event, big or small, I expect to make a minimum of three new, great connections.

When I have a conversation, I expect to either learn something valuable or contribute something valuable to somebody.

3. Take action and choose your words wisely.

> *"Try not. Do, or do not. There is no try."*
> —Yoda

In my corporate sales rep days, I'd often be driving my minivan for one to two hours to get to my next customer, so I listened to a lot of training CDs. I am so grateful a good friend of mine introduced me to Jim Rohn as a birthday gift, which completely changed my life.

The one thing that stuck with me was his *Law of Diminishing Intent*. He says:

"What separates the successful from the unsuccessful so many times is that the successful simply do it. They take action; they aren't necessarily smarter than others, they just work the plan. And the time to act is when the emotion is strong. We intend to act when the idea strikes us, when the emotion is high, but if we delay and we don't translate that into action fairly soon, the intention starts to diminish, and a month from now it's cold and a year from now it can't be found."—Jim Rohn

I started living by this law. When an opportunity arose and I had a good feeling about it, instead of waiting for the right moment, I would be in action right away. I knew that if I didn't, it might never happen. So now when I come across an event and it feels good, I will go without needing to know the details.

This applies to people I meet and those who I want to connect with again. I schedule my next conversation as soon as possible. So take immediate action if you are introduced to a hot lead or if you meet someone with whom you want to develop a long-term relationship. Schedule the next meeting immediately. One person can turn your business and your life around.

One of the best ways to practice networking is to network as you go. For me, I will say hello to people pretty much anywhere. I met one of my best hairdressers on a subway ride here in Toronto. On a recent trip to Utah, I met a woman sitting on the plane beside me. I said hello, we chatted, and I asked questions and listened. She is from San Diego, and it turned out that we had children of similar age and even one with the same name. We ended up meeting again when my family took a trip down to San Diego and she became one of my clients.

Again, it's taking action anytime, anywhere. I believe in living your dream now as opportunity is everywhere. When you meet people and you share what you are up to and you learn about them, not only is it good for business connections, but I assure you that it also helps you with fulfilling your goals and dreams.

Enjoy your Networking Journey. Start being more kind and grateful—and take action.

In gratitude,

Bonnie Chan

Quotes:

"Yesterday I was clever, so I wanted to change the world. Today I am wise, so I am changing myself."
—*Rumi*

"You can have everything in life you want, if you will just help enough other people get what they want."
—*ZigZiglar*

"Be who you are and say what you feel, because those who mind don't matter and those who matter don't mind."
—*Dr. Seuss*

"Your imagination is your preview of life's coming attractions."
—*Albert Einstein*

"The purpose of our lives is to be happy."
—*Dalai Lama*

"Change your thoughts and you change your world."
—*Norman Vincent Peale*

"Try not do, or do not. There is no try."
—*Yoda*

"Be thankful for what you have; you'll end up having more. If you concentrate on what you don't have, you will never, ever have enough"
—*Oprah Winfrey*

Bonnie Chan

Bonnie Chan is the founder of *Network to Grow*. Bonnie works with professionals and entrepreneurs to expand their client base and master the art of networking along with appreciation marketing. *Network to Grow* isn't just about having a continual stream of new clients and making a profit; it's also about building and nurturing relationships, self-development, and making a difference in the community with one's unique gifts and talents.

Bonnie received a Bachelor degree in Marketing from Simon Fraser University and has worked in various capacities in sales, marketing, and product sourcing with small start-up firms and Fortune 500 companies.

Bonnie is known as the "Networking Queen" among her friends and colleagues in Toronto. She will teach you how to incorporate networking and appreciation marketing into your already active schedule so that you can continually attract business success into your life. She adores her husband, Aaron, and two boys, Lucas and Jaden.

You can learn more about Bonnie on her website at www.networktogrow.com

My Three L.U.V Principles – Recipe for Success in Life and Love

By Carmelia Ray

Learn Unique Value

1. **The first step to success in anything you do is to learn everything there is to know about your passion and business.**

I entered the world of matchmaking in 1992 in my early twenties. I knew absolutely nothing about dating and relationships. The matchmaking industry was still foreign to a lot of people and online dating was not a "thing" back then. I was surprised to learn there was an actual business that helped people find love. The opportunity to work for a dating company really appealed to me. In fact, just before I was hired by a 172-office National matchmaking firm, Together Dating, I had ended a two-year toxic and abusive relationship. I was not lucky in love.

The road to success was not an easy one. I had a rough and rocky start which began in my teens. I ran away from home at the age of seventeen and spent a period of time homeless, sleeping from various friends' closets, couches, and living rooms. It was during my time away from home that I met this boy who I fell in love with. This was my first taste of heartbreak and I really took it badly. So when I had the chance to work in the matchmaking business, I said to myself, "Well, if I can't make love work for me, the least I could do was to learn how I could help others find love in their lives!"

Twenty-three years and 60,000+ conversations later with singles all over the world, I am now a well-known and widely sought after dating, matchmaking, and relationship expert, consulting and writing for top dating sites and the most successful matchmakers across the globe. People say it takes 10,000 or more hours to be considered an expert in your field. That's the equivalent of working forty hours a week over a five-year span. Richard Branson recently published his "Top 10 Illustrated Success Tips" on the Virgin Blog. I highly recommend you read all ten. He begins by stating, "I learn better through experience than theory." Much of his success tips had a similar theme; be in action towards your goal!

When you're in "action," the magic happens. You end up learning everything there is to know about your industry and the impact of the work you do. Learning, however, is much more than just the experiences you go through. I knew I had very little experience in the dating world when I started. I had no idea what to say to men and women who were twice my age back then. I was speaking with CEOs, accountants, professors, business owners, and serious entrepreneurs about their love lives. I worked in the call centre so I pretended I was in my thirties if they ever asked me how old I was. They were turning to me (how ironic) for love advice. Thank goodness for my mentors, my ability to build rapport and for call centre scripts! I had been given a scripted answer for almost any scenario or objection given to me. I was a very good listener and I could take instruction well. I was also a sponge and competitive by nature. In a room of over fifty telemarketers, I quickly became one of the youngest and top performers. Whatever training material and resources that were given to me, I studied them and took them home to learn even more after hours.

I recall my supervisor at the time would give me the oldest, coldest, and most challenging leads. I had to work with the lowest income earners, most skeptical types and I would turn them around into appointments. I was able to do this with what I had learned about the industry and the benefits of using a dating service. I had learned the art of rapport and asking the right questions. People instantly trusted me over the phone; I really wanted them to change their life. My principle job was to give information, screen and qualify a single person over the phone, and invite them in for an interview to learn about matchmaking. I was also working part-time at Coles bookstore when I started working in the dating industry. I used my spare time there to research and study anything I could about dating and becoming a better salesperson. My nose was deep into any material I could find to help me connect with singles and turn a "NO" into a "YES." It paid off because I put in the work and focused on learning the things I did not know in order to be the best I could be for the people I spoke with.

2. Know your unique abilities and your unique clients.

When I Google the word "unique" the first thing that comes up is this: "adj, being the only one of its kind; unlike anything else… particularly remarkable, special, or unusual."

Isn't it great to know that you are the only one of your kind; unlike anything else? Wow! I invite you to say that over and over again and really get that you're special; unlike anything else. It's such an empowering feeling when you begin to identify what's unique about yourself; what makes you really stand out from anyone else in the world; and more importantly, what is unique about you in your industry. When was the last time you really took stock of all of your unique abilities? I invite you to write down everything it is that you do in your day-to-day life. Write down what you do in your day-to-day work life, day-to-day love life, and day-to-day personal life. Your personal life may include your partner, your family, your immediate family, or your friends and colleagues. Write down a healthy list of positive character and personality traits. Here's a few to get you started:

I am funny

I am powerful

I am creative

I am honest

I see the good in others

I am optimistic

I love to encourage others

People seek me out for advice

I live a life I love

I would advise that you have at least five to ten identifiable and undeniable positive personality traits that are unique to you and your ability. This is what you will be known for and what you will live by. You are going to be in action and be the possibility of those key positive personality traits for yourself and for anyone around you. Isn't it an awesome feeling to know that you are creating passion? Or that you are being creative, optimistic, loyal, and confident? The real reward comes when you can identify what's unique about your clients and the people who are important to you! Consider how you can you help someone else recognize their unique ability and their awesomeness. Most people are quick to label someone with a negative character trait. We blame quickly and we make excuses for ourselves and for others. Imagine being someone who keeps your word, who lives with integrity, and who stands for others to live into their possibility. We would live in a very different world and it would be extraordinary. Mahatma Ghandi says, "Happiness is when what you say, what you think, and what you do are in Harmony." Identify your unique ability and discover what it is for others. We all want to feel special.

3. Give Value and Find Value in Others

In the world of dating and matchmaking, I find that people really do struggle with the value of finding love and with what they're willing to sacrifice, to do and to invest in it. Today's singles have the choice of so many free online dating sites and paid online dating sites. Singles today also have access to dating coaches, dating services, and boutique matchmakers. The investment to this higher end of boutique personal services can range from $10,000–$100,000+ in some cases. Patti Stanger has created a successful brand with the "Millionaire Matchmaker," and her show on Bravo proves the point of how much value love can be for some singles.

Value is really anything that people are willing to pay for what you're offering. Let's begin with giving value; how do you do that? First of all, if no one wants what you're offering, then the service or thing is worthless. Secondly, consider what's important to you and your life. Time is undeniably, a precious commodity. We all get the same amount of time to work with, but some of us value it more than others. Steve Jobs is quoted as saying:

> "Your time is limited, so don't waste it living someone else's life. Don't be trapped by dogma — which is living with the results of other people's thinking. Don't let the noise of others' opinions drown out your own inner voice. And most important, have the courage to follow your heart and intuition. They somehow already know what you truly want to become. Everything else is secondary."
> —Steve Jobs

I consider time to be my most valuable asset. Admittedly, I haven't always spent it wisely. Do you notice how many things can pull you away from the important tasks? Do you find yourself glancing at your newsfeed only to discover that ten minutes have passed by? Do you take into account the time you are spending with people and whether you're being productive or just making a lot of noise? Being efficient and being effective can have two very different outcomes. The key question to ask yourself is, "What difference am I making?" In other words, does spending time talking about what you're going to do—creating a well-executed "future" game plan—actually get results just "talking" about it? Be mindful of all the talking and focus more on the doing and being.

> "Leaders spend 5% of their time on the problem in 95% of their time on the solution. Get over it and crush it!"
> —Tony Robbins

Anyone who values their own time and activities will also value others. The funny thing is that some people fall into the trap of completely giving up their own time to make someone else's dreams come true. A great question someone asked me in a time when I was frustrated and unhappy with what I was up to was, "Is what you're doing RIGHT NOW, getting you OUT of what you're doing RIGHT NOW?" Imagine a life where you can spend time doing the things you love and the things that would make a real difference for others! It's can be very challenging for people to prioritize, and it's important that you really account for your time. I love what the Dalai Lama says about this concept.

> "Old friends pass away, new friends appear. It is just like the days.
> An old day passes, a new day arrives. The important thing is to
> make it meaningful: a meaningful friend—or a meaningful day."
> —Dalai Lama

You are the only person who knows your true worth and value. Be confident in the possibility of offering the best service to your clients. For most people in the service industry like myself, our clients are our most valuable asset. Acknowledge your clients for their part in making your dreams come true and include them in your journey. I am privileged to know so many helping professionals who are truly proud of the work they do and who value their worth and their loyal customers. Whatever it is that you're up to, know you're worth and live into your greatness!"

Carmelia Ray

Carmelia Ray is an online dating expert, matchmaker, and certified dating coach. She has personally interviewed over sixty thousand singles, and coaches singles to help find, attract, and keep their ideal partner. Carmelia is a published author, public speaker and sought after media personality in the world of dating and matchmaking. She teaches her clients powerful attraction, flirting, and communication tips to experience massive breakthroughs in their dating and relationship lives.

Carmelia co-produces and hosts "iDate", the largest online dating and matchmaking conference world wide. iDate gathers the executives and business owners in the online dating industry and the worlds leading dating professionals. She also serves as CMO at Instant Chemistry, a Toronto based bio tech company bringing genetic matchmaking to the world. Carmelia facilitates singles events in Toronto for Match.com and Lifemates Canada. She contributes expert dating & relationship content to several authoritative blogs and online dating sites such as eHarmony, Plenty of Fish and Best Dating Sites.

Carmelia is a powerful connector and networker. In her spare time she enjoys spending time with her 2 children, family and friends.

To learn more about Carmelia Ray visit: HYPERLINK "http://www.carmeliaray.com"www.carmeliaray.com

For dating and relationship advice visit her blog:www.datingloveandsextips.com

Connect with her socially on Facebook, Twitter, Instagram and LinkedIn @CarmeliaRay email:Carmeliaray@gmail.com

Defining Success
Live Life on Your Terms

By Crystal-Marie Sealy

Founder of Successiory (Inc) Social Media Consulting

My journey of entrepreneurship with Successiory (www.successiory.ca) has been one of courage and love. It hasn't been easy, but I chose to press on despite apparent failures. My advice is: don't quit, and you can be invincible. So you can't fly or teleport just yet, but in your quest to make your dreams reality, you are limited only by the limits you place on yourself.

Defining Success

Looking back, I've done a lot with my thirty-two years on this planet. As a perfectionist, I've never really seen myself as successful. No matter what I achieved my inner critic said, "You didn't do it as well as you could have" or "You should have done more." Can you relate to this?

Recently, my boyfriend remarked, "Complete is better than perfect." Success is not perfection. Sometimes success is as simple as getting out of our own way. Those in need of your help or services will suffer needlessly if you withhold it until you think you have reached your level of perfection.

Life, Perfectionism and Choices

I have always been introspective. Even as a child, I analyzed the "who, what, when, where, how, why, and what if" of every situation I faced.

By age 12, I'd planned my life; from dream house, business, husband, and children, to the atmosphere I'd create at home. If there was a "perfect" way, I'd find it—logically, not emotionally. At 20, I still couldn't see where emotions fit into the equation. Hopefully you're wiser. The emotional "you" can be a powerful ally.

I can't fit into one chapter the impact that perfectionism had on my passion for dance, writing, and drawing during those formative years. I regret not living out loud. Imagine being on stage, at the climax of everything you rehearsed. You are about to execute the choreography that makes the crowd feel the story, but you can't because your emotions weren't invited to the party. That hurt every time.

On family, I have a mother who would move Heaven and earth for me, a father who supports my entrepreneurial spirit, and a brother with whom I share an extra-sensory perception (ESP) connection. I have a huge, loving, extended family. Still, I ran away from home to feel free enough to live my dream.

Health for a Workaholic

At 23, I thought moving to Canada would be bliss, as I could finally live alone. Looking back, I think I found bliss because I came to Canada without overanalyzing it. I was free to simply *be*. Blissful recluse or not, I did a lot. I played softball, performed with a dance group for two years, and even got out to night clubs. Still, I ensured that I built a life that gave me the downtime I needed. Or so I thought.

Twenty-five and a workaholic, I kept getting overlooked for career opportunities. One manager pointed out that others were wary of the young woman the CEO hired, himself. I transferred to that manager's team. I enjoyed it, but I was still a workaholic. One day, I got home around 10 p.m. and blacked out. I woke up at 3 a.m. with a dent in my skull where my head hit the wall. I still have that dent! After that frightening and enlightening experience I decided to stop "working after work" and take better care of myself.

I began studying for my Master of Business Administration (MBA) at the Schulich School of Business, York University, at age 26. I applied to no other school because only Schulich offered strategy, entrepreneurship, and environmental sustainability specializations. In my second year, I was elected Communications Director of the Graduate Business Council (GBC) and fell in love with social media. I decided I would focus on social media and strategy consulting, and Successiory was born.

However, I crashed again one year later. I thought I was just exhausted, but one morning I was paralyzed. My tongue made a left hook in my mouth and froze. This lasted for about five minutes and I thought I was having a stroke! When I made it to the hospital, they could find nothing wrong. Again, I committed to taking care of myself and I promised myself that this time I'd stick with it.

A New Passion

At 25, I graduated at the tail end of the recession. I taught English as a second language (ESL) in Toronto to keep Successiory (Inc) going. I've always loved and excelled at languages and thought that teaching more than twenty students at a time would eliminate my intense dislike for public speaking. It did way more than that for me. I went home with my heart overflowing every day!

Teaching introduced me to another part of myself. I didn't realize how much I really loved people until then. I'm still in touch with hundreds of my former students from South Korea, Saudi Arabia, Germany, Spain, France, Brazil, China, Turkey, Vietnam, Japan, and so many other countries. They have all played a part in stretching my capacity to love. They awakened the free spirit in me.

Now or Never

You know how you almost never "feel" your age? Well, I am not sure why, but 30 was the only age that I really felt. My liberation decade began. I suddenly felt extremely powerful; I could do anything! Almost overnight, I felt truly comfortable in my own skin, and in June I left teaching in pursuit of a better salary. After a year of fruitless politics, the death of a dear colleague, and a boss who simply hated my very being, I'd had enough. For the third time I was getting seriously ill and again, the doctors didn't know what was wrong. No job was worth that, so I quit. It was then, at 31, that I realized the freedom of focusing solely on my business. For the first time in years, I had the time to work effectively and take care of myself.

Now, my path is my own. You have to follow your own path. If you need another job while building your business then get one, but if you can focus solely on your business, do it. Chart your own course. The pain of hunger and the "shame" of borrowing quickly taught me the importance of building a business that generates the money needed to live and keep the business alive.

My Journey Today

Today, Successiory (Inc) is focused on social media strategy for professional, service-based, solo entrepreneurs. They have a client base and embrace the values I outline in my lessons below. They understand the value of organic social media community in generating leads. Moreover, they recognize its value in helping them to stay connected with clients well beyond the moment when they first changed their lives. Whether they're busy, frustrated, or overwhelmed, the E.A.S.Y. Social Media Strategy 5-week program works because it delivers a strategy that is "effective, actionable, simple, yours" (E.A.S.Y.). It is a strategy that fits their schedules, leverages their strengths, and matches their technological comfort.

Why would this be what I dedicate my life to? My love for people has transformed itself into a strong passion for being the mirror that helps clients see the beauty and value of their authentic brand persona. When they embrace that, those who need them will finally see and embrace it, as well. Social media is about community. Marketing, PR, HR—sure, but it is community first, and in community it is the human connection that matters. I help bring that to life.

What about you? What do you do? Why?

Lessons I Keep Learning

1. Value Yourself

I am a morning person and a recovering workaholic. As a result, I learned to set feasible deadlines and stop at 4 p.m. each day. My weekends are off limits and I work with my energy levels. I do 70 percent solo work and 30 percent collaborative work. I am learning to say "no" without guilt or explanation. People push against these boundaries, but I choose to value myself, each time.

Put boundaries in place to protect what you value. You lock your front door, right? Aren't you also priceless? What are your boundaries and values? When are your most productive hours? Are you better working solo or collaborating with others? Learn and respect your own boundaries; they make you more effective. Try this for one month: Set an alarm, and at the same time each day revisit your most recent thought or interaction. Were you being yourself, and authentic? Track your progress.

Stretch yourself, yes. Take opportunities. Just be true to yourself. Do not say yes to tasks or events that you'll be too tired to do well, otherwise both you and your colleagues will wind up suffering.

For reinforcement, check out *"the Big Enough Company"* by Adelaide Lancaster and Amy Abrams (http://ingoodcompany.com/book) and the blog post *"Back to Basics - Your Approval Required"* (http://protectyourdreams.blogspot.ca/2014/07/back-to-basics-your-approval-required.html).

2. Money Matters—What is Your Number?

Money is ubiquitous, but you need to have it. You can't help anyone if your business is not sustainable. Invest in yourself and connect with others who do the same. How much do you need to keep your business afloat? How much do you need to sustain the lifestyle you want? Are your services worth that? If not, offer the premium version of your service that does, and connect with clients who can, and will, pay for it. Fact: You literally can't afford to provide a service for "whatever prospects can afford" simply because they "need it." You learn very quickly that if you go out of business, they'll just find someone else. So: What is your number?

3. You Can Do It Alone but You Don't Have To

You will be alright on your own, but the right community is priceless. The reason many of us "do it alone" is because we can't seem to find trustworthy people who support our goals. I believe the right community is out there. If you're true to yourself, you'll recognize those who you're compatible with and who you can trust. Make time to build the right community. No one person will meet all of your needs, but they may all have a piece of the puzzle. Who makes up your community?

For me, my family has been crucial. As well, Carol Schulte (www.carolschulte.com) got me off my derrière. Jason Reid (www.rechargemymojo.com) asked, "What is your number" and shaped my signature talk. Dan Blackburn (www.danblackburn.com) helps me to stay true to my "why." Christine Cirka (facebook.com/EssencetoSuccess) got me to assess my beliefs around money. Réjeanne Aimey, Co-Founder (www.embodyfeminine.ca) helped me to extend visualization to all of my senses. Odette Laurie (www.businesswomenontop.com) got me to commit to taking action today, instead of "one day."

Who echoes your internal truths? Who keeps you going when you can't? Start with one person.

Your Turn to Take Action

I believe you were born at exactly the right time, in the right generation, country, city and physical body, because you are exactly what both you and the world need right now. Celebrate that!

Enjoy the journey. Stories you hear about people finally getting what they dreamed of and then being sorely disappointed sometimes stem from the fact that they didn't enjoy the journey. The fulfillment you find at the end of your journey can be very small without the joys along the way.

Your dream is not too big or too lofty. It's worth it. Choose to start today with one small step. Even if you're tired and unfocused, start. Your dreams will wake you up and keep you going.

Testimonials

"Crystal-Marie Sealy is a courageous and intelligent woman who is inspirational in her outlook and her focus. Reading her story has allowed me to appreciate the circumstances that made her the way she is. Her stories of perfectionism and passion are instantly relatable for me, as is her determination for sustainable physical and spiritual health. I see the characteristics of the true 21st Century entrepreneur in her—independent, self-motivated, responsible and generous. I know her success will make the world a better place."

*Jason Reid, Author, Speaker, Business Coach
Founder of the R.I.C.H. Zone & the Rechargeable Entrepreneur
(www.rechargemymojo.com)*

"This is a very interesting and personal story! Now I know a lot more about your background and how you got to where you are now. I thought you had a very good flow throughout your story, which led up to your final three learning points for your readers. As I was reading along, I was compelled by your life journey and when it got to the third "and then I crashed again" part, I was almost saying out loud "Oh no!" And that is a good sign of a compelling story."

*Martina V. Rowley, Virtual Assistant
Founder & Manager of Beach Business Hub
(www.beachbusinesshub.ca)*

Crystal-Marie Sealy

Crystal-Marie Sealy, MBA, is the president and founder of the boutique social media strategy consulting firm, *Successiory (Inc)* in Toronto, Canada. Driven by her passion to connect others and to empower entrepreneurs to streamline operations so they can do more in less time and have time to live life, Crystal-Marie has developed the E.A.S.Y. Social Media Strategy Program. This five-week course is dedicated to empowering service-based entrepreneurs with the ability to create a sustainable client social media community that fits their busy schedules. She has saved some clients up to 460 hours a year. The goal is always to focus social media strategy on the right community—client community—those who truly need, value, and invest in you.

More importantly, like you, Crystal-Marie is a normal person who wanted more for those around her. A career that began in 2001 in ecology and environmental sciences is an interesting one. It took her through an ongoing love for ecology that expanded into a passion to empower people through communications. Her business degree changed from Entrepreneurial Strategy and Marketing communications in 2009, to the niche of social media strategy for entrepreneurs.

Connect with Crystal-Marie at Successiory and learn more by visiting her website at http://www.successiory.ca

The Road to Success is Not Always Paved

By Dana Janzen

Ask one hundred people to define success, and you'll probably get one hundred different answers. Each person has their own notion of success. For some, success is equated with wealth. For others, success comes in the form of personal fulfillment. My definition of success is more akin to scaling a mountain than gaining fame and fortune.

As a leadership coach and performance consultant, I have the privilege of partnering with my clients as they transform their companies, businesses, and careers by focusing on their own unique paths to success. It's immensely gratifying and humbling to be invited into people's lives as they embark upon their journeys of growth and development. It's clear to me that everyone seeks success in a different way. But if I had to name the one common denominator—the proverbial pot of gold everyone is seeking—it's fulfillment.

For me, it's the deep sense of satisfaction that comes from attaining a goal—something I've worked tirelessly and relentlessly to achieve. Something that provokes a healthy dose of excitement along with a touch of fear. These aren't just any goals. They're Big, Hairy, Audacious Goals (BHAG). Coined by author and management guru Jim Collins, the term describes a relentless drive for progress and innovation.

I'm a big believer in the power of BHAGs. They set visionary leaders and organizations apart. According to Collins, "The power of the BHAG is that it gets you out of thinking too small." In my own life, and as a leadership coach, Big Hairy Audacious Goals have been an indispensable tool for personal and professional transformation. To succeed, your vision and goals need to be crystal clear. As do your motivations. Why are your vision and goals important to you? If they're not deeply personal and compelling, you won't be motivated to achieve them.

I'm continuously setting new goals and challenges, gaining valuable experience and confidence along the way. I've discovered a lot about myself: what I excel at and where my talents lie—and how to leverage the two to achieve success.

Life has taught me many lessons. Let me share a few that may help as you pursue your own path to success.

Unleash Your Inner Daredevil

> *"If we're growing, we're always going to be out of our comfort zone."*
> —John C. Maxwell (author and leadership expert)

I jumped into my first entrepreneurial experience armed with a Big Hairy Audacious Goal and a sense of adventure. I tried something new and ended up having a rewarding and formative experience.

During my third year of university, I noticed posters around campus inviting students to open their own student painting franchise. They promised summer earnings of eight to ten thousand dollars, possibly more. My first thought was, "I could never do that!" But every time I walked by one of those posters, I began to think, "Could I?" and then, "Why not?"

For someone without any entrepreneurial experience, it was an intimidating and challenging proposition. It required thousands of dollars upfront for the car and equipment I would need to give my venture a shot at success—a huge investment for a full-time student. What if I didn't succeed? What if I didn't make any money? How would I pay for next year's tuition? After speaking with a number of people who had already owned and run their own franchises (with varying degrees of success and failure), I took the plunge. In the wise words of the late author and psychologist Susan Jeffers, I decided to "feel the fear and do it anyway."

This so-called summer job started in February, as I lay the ground work for the busy summer season ahead. I spent countless hours learning business basics, and everything from how to paint, to how to hire a team of students. I took out loans to invest in the car and equipment I would need, hired my first crew—my younger brother and his friends—and then advertised in the newspaper (this was pre-Internet).

Day in and day out, I cold called, knocked on people's doors, conducted job estimates, and learned to close the deal. In addition to honing my sales technique, I gained invaluable business experience. I successfully managed my team of student painters. I hired. I fired. I hired again. I learned how to deal with unmotivated employees and acrimonious team dynamics. I resolved customer issues. And I kept myself motivated all the while. Each morning, I awoke with a sense of fear. If I didn't make it happen, no one would!

When my painting venture wrapped up in October, I breathed a huge sigh of relief. I ended up earning ten thousand dollars, and a great deal of pride. I walked away armed with a ton of experience: making business decisions, managing bottom-line profit, lessons on hiring good people, motivating teams, prospecting and closing business, and how to deal with customers of all kinds. Best of all, I expanded my view of what I was capable of. If I could take on something like that and succeed, I could do anything!

Was it easy? Absolutely not! I was terrified and uncomfortable. But when I look back upon that summer, it was an amazing and fulfilling experience. I learned new skills and developed business insights that I've put to good use throughout my career. Most importantly, I realized that I can do anything I focus on—with an extra dose of courage.

You are capable of more than you know. How high would you set your sights if failure wasn't an option?

GET A LIFE!

It's easy to lose focus on your personal life when you're so hard at work pursuing your goals. But when faced with a setback—and let's face it, they happen to us all—having meaningful interests outside of work will give you something to fall back on. More than that, they'll sustain your focus and momentum so you can continue on your path to success. When faced with a challenge early on in my career, I looked inward and discovered new skills and talents that continue to inspire me and help achieve balance in my life.

Early in my career, I worked in the financial industry selling mortgages, mutual funds, and giving financial advice to banking customers. Because of my outgoing personality and knack for selling, my uncle thought I'd be a good fit in the pharmaceutical industry. At the time, I knew absolutely nothing about the industry. Over the next eight months, I phoned friends and contacts, and networked my way to my first Pharmaceutical Sales Representative job with a large, global pharmaceutical company. My territory was an eight-hour driving radius with no existing customer lists and minimal past representation. I was on the road constantly, often getting by on little sleep as I visited doctors' offices and created a solid list of specialist physicians whom I targeted.

I absolutely loved my job. And I was great at it. I watched my sales grow, along with the importance of work in my life. Quickly, the job became my life.

As luck would have it, the division I worked for was sold off after only ten months into the job. As the most junior employee, I was let go. I was devastated. I panicked! I didn't know what to do with myself when I wasn't working and traveling eighteen hours a day. I'd come to view myself strictly through the lens of my job. I was my job. My job was me.

I hit the ground looking for work and meeting with head-hunters, but quickly realized there were many more hours in the day to fill. With what? Other than fitness, I didn't have any hobbies.

Like many people facing unemployment, I was anxious and scared. I was ashamed that I'd lost my job—even though I was a good employee. I needed an outlet; something to distract me from my disappointment. So I turned to cooking shows and started to flex my creative muscle by experimenting in the kitchen. Before I knew it, I was making bagels from scratch! As the renowned workaholic among my friends, it was unusual to see me cultivate my personal interests. It felt amazing to expand my horizons and do more than one focused thing, day in and day out.

Within three months, I was scooped up by my previous competitor and the market leader. While my unemployment only lasted a short time, I have continued to strive for balance in my life. When I have other interests, it gives my mind a break and makes me happier. This allows me to be better, more focused, and more productive in my work life.

Take it from me. Don't let your career define you. If you have no interests outside of work, get curious and ask questions! Do yourself the great favor of discovering what it is you're passionate about. Where do your hidden talents lie?

Step Up and Be Your Own Leader

> *"To be yourself in a world that is constantly trying to make you something else is the greatest accomplishment."*
> —Ralph Waldo Emerson

I've always been a high performer. I take great pride in excelling at whatever I set my mind to. Ten years after being laid off, I was the top sales performer, winning many sales awards and promotions. My hard work and success were recognized with a promotion to a national marketing role. This is what I had worked tirelessly towards. I should have been happy, but I wasn't. Being stuck behind a desk all day running forecasts was not a good fit. I was bored. I'm a people person—I needed to be face to face, interacting with people.

So I switched paths to a business consulting position where I excelled with customers. I was in my element; so much so that I was promoted to lead a team of professionals—a group of my former peers. I was spending 50 per cent of my time on administrative work, and another 30 per cent of my day adult babysitting and putting out fires, which left me little time to coach my team and interact with customers. I was miserable! How could that be? Promotion after promotion, I was on the fast track to success. It just wasn't the right track for me.

My team was expanding and I was recruiting another business consultant. As I signed off on the job posting, I had an epiphany. That was the job I wanted! That was the job I excelled at, which enabled me to leverage my skills and strengths. I wanted to go back, but the idea of demoting myself was mortifying. Had I worked so hard to advance up the corporate ladder, only to take two steps back?

I approached my boss and expressed how unhappy I was. The good will and relationship equity I had built up over the years meant they were eager to retain me and keep me happy. And happy I was. I ended up negotiating a return to the role I loved and was great at—a demotion on paper, but not in terms of my fulfillment. Sure, I had to swallow my pride, but I absolutely made the right decision.

It's never easy to forge your own path, to stop climbing the proverbial corporate ladder and do what's *right* for you—not what's expected of you. When I took the time to analyze my talents and interests, I realized my path to success wasn't going to be linear. Climbing the corporate ladder just wasn't for me—the jungle gym is more my style! It took courage to do the unexpected and stay true to my strengths and my passions, instead of continuing along the wrong path and marching like a soldier in the corporate game.

Stop for a moment. Are you being a corporate soldier in your life? Decide which path is *truly* best for you. Consider choosing the unpaved road.

D. Dana Janzen

D. Dana Janzen is a Toronto-based leadership coach and performance consultant. She partners with business owners, leaders, and their teams to accelerate their success by focusing on their core asset: people. It's through effective leadership and high performing teams that companies meet—and exceed—their strategic goals, all while fostering a positive and sustainable corporate culture enjoyed by employees and customers alike.

Dana's expertise is often sought after to increase employee engagement and retention, create a problem-solving mindset, and improve team communication and performance management. This directly impacts the customer experience, driving loyalty, referrals, and business growth.

She brings over twenty years of corporate and small business experience in the areas of business consulting, coaching, influence, team building, leadership development, people and performance management, communication, customer service best practices, sales, and marketing. An Honors Business graduate of Wilfred Laurier University, Dana has a passion for people and for how they operate in business and in life. She's completed adult learning courses at University of Toronto (OISE), is a member of the ICF (International Coach Federation), and an ATC (Adler Trained Coach). Dana is an avid athlete, artist, and enthusiastic participant in life. She owns the boutique firm, *Coaching 4 Results*.

When You Almost Die, You Wake Up

By Fahad Buchh

Imagine. You are nine years old. The last thing you remember is the world spinning, going dark and then falling. The first thing you hear is a machine beeping, strange clicking sounds. You become aware of something up your nose and that air is coming out of it. As you open your eyes, they slowly focus on the sterile sheen of the hospital room.

When I was nine years old, I went through a life-changing experience; I almost died due to extreme high fevers. My body temperature was at 105°+. My parents, panic-stricken, rushed me to the hospital and they saved my life. The doctors said that I had just survived by a few minutes. I was unaware of all of this. When I woke up the next morning in the hospital, I was surprised. The first words that came out of my mouth were, "Where am I?" It might seem surprising, but somehow my nine-year-old brain registered a deep knowing, "I have been given another chance!" Equally surprising was that my nine-year-old brain immediately understood the enormity of that meaning. Something changed inside me. Something beyond the knowing of an ordinary nine year old. I was extremely grateful for this opportunity. Suddenly, I was ready to face the world; face the world in a very grown up way.

The doctors, worried about another episode, played it safe and put me on medication for the next three years. They said that I needed to limit myself from physical activities and sports. After this incident, I struggled in school. My parents, society, and everyone else told me I had a lot of time to live. So, I never worried about it. After this incident, I realized that life is short. I thought that I really didn't have much time left. I made a decision that day, a decision I have lived with ever since. I decided to never ever blame the world for my problems. I needed to find a way no matter what happened. This illness created a deep realization within me. I needed to make a difference in the world. After that day, my life completely changed. I began take risks. I stopped playing it safe. I thought that I didn't have much time; I started looking for new opportunities. I respected every precious minute I was living.

A few weeks after the incident, I was walking in my local mall and I saw that a non-profit organization was giving away free Pokémon badges for a promotion. I quickly ran and grabbed two large packages. I had a great idea. Why don't I sell these badges to kids? Immediately, my old mindset told me, "No, don't do that." But, then the memories of my recent experience reminded me of how short life can be and my new mindset said, "Take *big* risks." For a moment, I thought about asking my friends for advice. That would have been a wise decision. But, when I told them what I was thinking, they made fun of me. They thought the idea was stupid, and no one would buy the badges. That got me fired up and excited. I knew then and there that when you are about to act on a new decision, start a new business, or make a new move, there will be people who laugh and make fun of you. However, I believed in me. I held my experience of near death close to me. I decided to take action.

So, I got on my little bicycle and went up to kids in my school ground. I started presenting my first product. My first heroic approach had little success; it resulted in a net profit of only thirty dollars. Not bad for a nine-year-old kid, right? I wanted to do better. I decided to change my strategy. Instead of approaching kids, who hardly had any money with them, I went door-to-door selling the cards to parents. This new strategy was a major success. I made ninety dollars on my first night. I sold all of my cards within four days and made a profit of two hundred dollars. I used some of the money I earned to purchase food to feed a homeless cat. The rest of the money I donated to feed homeless people in my community. I loved helping others.

It was in that moment that my mission in life was revealed to me. I love to make a difference in the lives of other people around me. My friends thought that I was just lucky. What most people don't know is that I was determined and persistent. I heard more "no's" than "yes's". I was told "no" 150 times before I heard my first "yes!" It looked like instant success, but that was just an illusion. Don't fall for that illusion! I proved all my friends wrong, and learned a great lesson. I was sure that in life I would come across ridicule again. The trick was to not react to the gossip and to the haters. Instead, I would respond by taking the first step toward what scares me the most. Whenever I have to decide between two options, I always pick the one that scares me the most.

Later, at the age of 14, I decided to take on another mighty challenge. The memory of my near-death experience was alive within me. I made a decision to play men's field hockey and represent my high school. I tried out and successfully made the team. I was extremely delighted and scared. Yikes! I had never ever played field hockey before. Imagine how you would feel if you had to represent your school playing a sport you never played before?

I was curious and I had a good attitude. I practiced every day for sixty days with a great coach. After hours and hours of hard work, dedication, and practice, it was time to prove myself. The big tournament was finally here. I travelled with my team for two hours to get to our destination. I was excited, but to be honest, I was nervous. I played relentlessly. I won the under-fifteen championship. But, that wasn't enough. I always wanted to go the extra mile. I knew that I could do more, be more and have more. I courageously went up to my coach and asked him to put me in, on the under-eighteen team. The pressure was enormous. I just kept telling myself, "The thing that scares me the most is the one I need to pursue." I could face being ridiculed by my colleagues, if I did not perform well. After all, this was nothing compared to death. I have always kept that near-death experience close to me. The result was that I ended up scoring a goal in the under-eighteen championship.

The secret formula I used was simple, "I just expected it." I expected myself to score. In life, we don't get anything we just want, but we get anything and everything we expect. My team lost the tournament. As usual, I was not satisfied with just scoring one goal. I wanted to know, "What else could I do?" I wanted to win in a bigger way. So, I decided I would come back next year and win the championship. In every great success story, there is hard work behind the glamorous results. When I made the decision, I had no doubt in my mind that I would accomplish my goal. I put my words into action and I practiced three hours every day for the next year.

There were times I wanted to quit, skip practice, and just take it easy. But, what kept me going was that I wanted to make my whole school proud by winning the championship. I wanted to inspire new young players to join the team.

Sometimes, life seems complicated. This is due to the fact that we have many options to choose from. Life has its ups and downs. One thing that we can keep in mind is that we always have a choice. I invite you to take on my challenge, to do the thing you are most afraid to do. Twitter #MrEnergizer. The things that we fear the most challenge us and help us grow into stronger and better human beings. Ask yourself this question, "What activity challenges me the most?" Share your responses on Twitter and Facebook. I could have settled for the one goal I scored in the first game, or for just making thirty dollars. But, I didn't.

Instead, I raised my standards, aimed high, and worked hard with all my energy and played in the tournament. As a result, I won the championship.

Now, if I were to describe in one word how my win made me feel, I would say it was "motivating." Wins in life are the biggest motivators we have. When in doubt, remember your wins. Simply close your eyes and feel how you felt at that moment. I always focus on my wins; I expect to win and I do win every time. I learned a lesson from my past experiences, that one should live each day abundantly and make the best of it. Although I am in perfectly good health now, my childhood incident changed my life in a positive way.

Here are the 12 steps I use to stay fully alive, take risks and keep winning:

1. I take complete responsibility for my life—I stop all blame games and take 100 per cent responsibility for every result I get. Start now and don't wait for tomorrow. We are the creators of our circumstances.

2. I see every circumstance as an illusion—my mental mindset is to see real life as a video game. Once we start seeing every situation with this mindset, there is no fear of rejection or loss in our minds. Have this as a motto: "I care, but not so much." This mindset helped me sell and make money. I did not care if I made the sales or not. What mattered most was having fun.

3. Scarcity can be a good thing if you use it to your advantage. Time is valuable; each day is a blessing. You will never get back each day. Take the first step toward your goals every day.

4. Be the most optimistic person you know. Don't join the "Not-Bad-Club." When I ask most individuals how they are doing, they say, "Not bad." Always reply with enthusiasm and a great attitude. This is very important! An optimistic attitude rubs off on other people like great computer software. However, if we choose to be pessimistic, it can be a bad mind-virus.

5. Be absolutely certain about your goals. In other words, expect it to happen. Everyone called me lucky when I made two hundred dollars, but luck is the effect of your internal thought process.

6. Have a reason bigger than yourself. A BIG reason can act as a cushion when things get tough. Your mission in life should drive you. I've never looked back; my mission keeps driving me forward to this day.

7. Keep the fire alive. Love the process of success and don't fall in love with the illusion of the end results. Raise your standards and have a desire to succeed, to do and accomplish more. Going door-to-door was a challenge, but I overcame it with an intense hunger to be successful and make an impact on other human beings. I learned that I needed to keep pushing when all the odds were against me.

8. Find your groove. What songs hit you the hardest? Every good song has a rhythm to it and life also has a similar rhythm. You just have to discover your own rhythm internally. Simply play your favorite song and notice how you feel. That feeling is your inner rhythm. Every activity you engage in must bring this inner groove to the table. This is how I found my strength, even when all the odds were against me. You can do the same just knowing that every activity has a groove to it. You must align your natural groove with the activity you are doing.

9. Maintain your excellence. Once you find your groove, it's important that you consistently feel this groove each minute of your life. Every minute of my life I play the role of a lead hero in my own movie. I feel like a winner and it helps me conquer every barrier you can imagine.

10. Let your dialogue serve you. I speak very highly of myself to myself. It's unbelievable how well I speak of myself to myself. Every human being is having a dialogue with themselves all the time. Ask yourself this question, "Is the story I tell myself every day serving me or is it making me weaker?"

11. Our successes are our foundation, not the end result. Imagine the tallest tower in the world, Burj Khalifa, on a cloudy day. You can't see the top of the building. When we start our journey from the bottom, it's important to remember that when we get to our goals we must continue our journey and never stop being satisfied with what we have become. If we have become generous as human beings then it's important to build on that success and keep going. Become even more generous, never stop. Most people think small. Are you thinking too small? Aim high and don't apologize for it.

12. Plan your legacy. Where will you be fifty years from now? Will you matter? Will you have inspired lives because of the work you did? What will you have done for the next generation? I ask these questions to myself every day. I make all my decisions based on these questions. I only take part in activities that will help me create a meaningful legacy. Fahad Buchh has been reported as saying:

"You will face challenges in life. Make sure you work hard and strive;
Live a life of purpose and passion. Do all that with compassion."

Fahad Buchh

Fahad Buchh solves business and focus challenges. His goal is to help his clients become more self-reliant, self-confident, and self-aware with his practical real world experience of being a young, successful entrepreneur.

Buchh energizes audiences with inspiring keynote presentations that motivate people to identify and pursue their highest aspirations. Fahad helps his audiences reconnect with their true motivation, their core values, and the creativity they need to take their performance to the next level.

You can contact Fahad Buchh
Personal Email - fahad@fahadbuchh.com
Twitter - https://twitter.com/fahadbuchh/
Instagram - http://instagram.com/fahadbuchh/

Forbes Riley's Remedy: Overcome to $uccess

By Forbes Riley

You are the sum of the obstacles you overcome: If you are lucky to live long enough, you're likely to go through some pretty bad stuff, whether it's the death of loved ones, losing all of your money or possessions, sickness and injuries, and other traumatic events. At best, you find that you come out of it—you've lived through some horrible circumstances or even seemingly improbable near-death experiences, and you discover yourself on the other side of it. You also realize that some people don't make it through similar circumstances, literally, by not escaping death or succumbing to suicide, but here you are, you made it through.

The powerful thing about living through the horrible times isn't just in the survival. I have learned that when you come through a personal tragedy, you come through different. Life is never about what happens to you; instead it is about how you choose to handle the hand you've been dealt. Under the same circumstances handed to two different people, one shuts down, wallows in self-pity, succumbs to fear, and uses their hardships as an excuse, while the other takes the challenge head-on, gets up, pushes back, and uses their forcefulness in pain as their entire motivation to persevere with all their might—and may come out on the other end as a multi-millionaire.

It isn't only about the single obstacle, either—how you show up and respond during the most gut-wrenching times of your life seems to add up. The more you succumb to fear, the further you seem to sink; whereas the more you handle your trials with a sense of perseverance and grace, the more powerful and successful you tend to become. This might also lend to building wisdom, helping you avoid some pitfalls while also helping you build an arsenal of skills to better deal with the next heartbreak coming your way.

This is a reoccurring lesson in my life that has ultimately lead me to build several highly successful businesses from my acting career, become the two billion dollar TV host, a world-traveled keynote speaker and professional coach and, most importantly, an incredibly proud mom to a pair of amazing twins. I've overcome everything from the death of both of my parents within a short period of time of one another, several near-death experiences including the 9/11 disaster, the murder of my husband's younger brother Dexter, the sudden death of one of my business partners, and many other lesser traumas and trials. When going through each of these experiences, they were all uniquely horrific. However, I got through them—stronger, wiser, and more determined than ever to succeed and persevere.

Leap and the net will appear. There's a joke among magicians—a young boy goes to his parents, who are both doctors, and he asks them what they think he should be when he grows up. His parents tell him, "Well, son, you should be a magician." Said no parent ever. As parents, we want more than anything for our children to feel safe and to be safe, and too often that can result in us giving horrible advice such as, "Honey, it's okay if you want to follow your dream to be a rock star, but you should have a Plan B in case that doesn't work out. Why don't you go to school to become an accountant?" As though this child who dreams of being a rock star should be perfectly happy as an accountant. I get it—the parents are thinking, well at least it's safe. He can get a secure job with benefits, develop a respectable skill that is widely needed, and so on.

But I ask you, how safe are you if you never dare to live your dreams? You're not safe from depression, stagnation, dissatisfaction, or regret. I promise you that those are serious problems that can fester and grow until they turn a person bitter and angry, causing havoc in relationships with family, friends, and at work. Also, what is a "secure job?" People get fired and laid off all the time. That seems to be a false sense of security if you ask me.

In my opinion, not only should you *not* have a Plan B, but Plan Bs are dangerous, can lead to self-sabotage at worst, and at best can be serious distractions from allowing you to ever create the life of your dreams or to live your fullest potential. If you never take risks, always attempt to "play it safe," and fail to dedicate yourself to your passion, or at least your insatiable curiosity, I think that you cheat yourself by failing to live life fully. It just doesn't make sense to me that you wouldn't live out your dream—this is your life right now, and now is all you have for sure, so go out and give your dream 100 per cent of your effort. And if you have a Plan B, throw it out because if you spend any time at all on your Plan B you cannot possibly give 100 per cent to your passion, and less than 100 per cent is not good enough. You're better than that, and you deserve better than that.

If you worry about the net and don't take the leap, nothing great is likely to happen. But if you go out, say this is what I want and I'm going to get it no matter what, and you take that leap—that's when dreams start to manifest. Knowing what you want is critical, too. I have a philosophy that if most people were to get one chance to stand before a genie to have one wish granted, they wouldn't know what to ask for, and that's because most people have no idea what they really want. If you don't know what you want, go figure it out. Dare to be bold, claim your passion, then go out and get it. This magical thing happens when you are crystal clear about what you want—the how to get it starts coming into focus, and you see opportunities and blessings everywhere. That's not to say that it's an easy road, but it's a clear path. You'll come upon obstacles, you'll get knocked down, and you'll even screw up—maybe even a lot—along the way. But if you continue to show up every day and do your part to fulfill your dream, you'll find that what you need will just be before you—the tools, resources, and opportunities just show up. The net appears.

In my life I leap and take risks all the time, and I'm not only more secure financially and otherwise than many people, but I know I look forward to always having more opportunities to leap. In fact, I live for those opportunities. My family's financial livelihood depends on my embracing these moments with everything I have. My personal security is realized by forever leaping. I've never had a "job" in my life—for me jobs are always ending: a movie, a TV show, an infomercial, a speaking gig, coaching retainers—these all come in finite intervals, and they are all scheduled to end on purpose. I am always out of a job and starting anew, and leaping. Through it all, one thing I can tell you for sure is that life's not long enough to have a Plan B.

How you do something is how you do everything. People think that they can lie to other people and to themselves about who they are and how they go about their lives. If you are a neat and organized person, your life will be neat and organized. If you are a mess, your life will be a mess. But, it goes deeper than that. You can tell a lot about a person by noticing how they do things: how messy they keep their car, how their clothes are put together, the shape of their nails and hair, how they write an email, how they speak and the words they choose, whether or not they follow through on promises, if they make excuses, complain, or are argumentative and contrary, or if they seek out ways to find common ground, solutions, and cooperate with others. These are all powerful tales about a person. Beyond being able to decipher if a person is messy or organized, it also says a lot about integrity. Does what they say match what you see?

There are two other well-known phrases that relate to this:

1) "If you want to know a person, pay attention to what he does and ignore what he says."

2) "When people show you who they are, believe them."

This concept is not only about deciphering the motivations of other people, but also of ourselves. "How you do something is how you do everything" is an important tool for personal checks and balances. Ask yourself, "Are my behaviors and habits consistent with the person I am?" If yes, great. If no, it's time to take inventory of your life and priorities and get your act back together. Be honest in all you do, and be mindful of dishonesty from others. We can all have moments of discombobulation, missteps, mistakes, and mishaps. However, it is our actions and behaviors that truly define who we are from every level of our existence. Clean out that closet, commit to keeping your car organized and maintained, seek out opportunities to be playful with others, and to find ways to come together as a team when you're faced with opposing views. At every level, be authentic and live a life of personal integrity.

Each of these bits of wisdom I have learned, reinforced, and relearned time and time again through the very first one: "You are the sum of the obstacles you overcome." Wisdom is not about knowledge so much as it is about continuous application and depth of knowledge. The most important lessons in life, I believe, is that you are required to learn them more than once, and then the lessons learned hit a deeper cord each time. The more fully you live, the more obstacles you overcome, and the more hardship you push through, the more leaps of faith you take to live the life of your dreams, the greater your depth and personal accountability towards integrity, and how you go about doing everything in your life, then the richer your life will become. My greatest gifts by far in all of my life are my son and daughter twins, Ryker and Makenna, and they are also my greatest teachers. Through them, every day, I am reminded of all I have learned in my life and also of how much I can still learn, love, and live. No matter how much professional and financial success I may achieve in this world, nothing beats that. Give more than you take, fake it till you make it, and enjoy this journey called life as it's a shorter rollercoaster than you imagine!

www.ForbesRiley.com

www.ForbesFactor.com

www.SpinGym.com

Forbes Riley

"You are the sum of the obstacles you overcome," Forbes frequently says as she turns her dreams into reality time and again. From launching her career as an actress on Broadway, film, and television to launching her own fitness and health empire and film and production studio, Forbes is committed to manifesting dreams.

Riley is recognized internationally as an award-winning two billion dollar TV host, spokesperson, celebrity fitness and lifestyle expert, professional coach, keynote speaker, actress, and author. She brings forth a clear message to empower people to dream bigger and bolder, and to work to achieve their dreams.

Forbes lives her mission that health and fitness is a lifestyle and not a fad. While she is considered a wild success in her professional career paths, she counts her greatest success of all to be her family. Forbes is the very proud mother of boy and girl twins, Ryker and Makenna, whom Forbes raises with her husband and business partner, Tom Riley, in their bi-coastal homes in St. Petersburg, FL and Los Angeles, CA.

www.facebook.com/ForbesRileyFANpage
Twitter: @forbesriley
Instagram: Forbes_Riley

Have a Little Faith

By Gillian Faith

Being asked to provide a written account of why people look to you for inspiration and what pieces of wisdom you would want to pass on is a humbling experience. It gives you pause for reflection on your life and an opportunity to reflect back on the people, times, and experiences in your life.

I know when I was first asked to be part of this incredible collection of inspirational people to create this anthology, I took several days to consider what I have to offer that others would find to be insightful and beneficial in their journey. The narrowing down of what I hoped to share to three specific pieces of wisdom has, in fact, changed over the course of several months. The enormous honor of being selected among so many other outstanding individuals who inspire, motivate, lead, and create change has been humbling.

It is with much joy and anticipation that I have chosen three nuggets of wisdom, which over the course of my life and as of recent, have had significant impact. I believe in these and should we meet at any of my events, a mutual event, which I certainly hope we do or somewhere in the future, I would love to share more about them with you.

The three nuggets of wisdom that I would like to share with you are:

The belief that...

1. Integrity is integral to everything we do in life. It is how we relate to others and keep ourselves accountable, and it's the lens through which we can better see the world.

The belief that...

2. Respect is given, not earned because there will always be people and situations in our life and in the world that never learned what respect is. Respect is something that must be taught, shown, and demonstrated with compassion, kindness, and understanding. When we teach and give respect it will be mutually reciprocated.

The belief that...

3. You must follow your heart and take risks when everyone else says that the idea is silly, doesn't make sense, or you will be rejected. Everyone is born with unique gifts, abilities, and talents, and pursuing those even when the odds are stacked against you only makes the outcome that much more rewarding.

Nugget 1: Integrity is Integral

I chose to share integrity first as one of my nuggets of wisdom because it comes from a very personal place and is foundational to every other nugget. Following the death of my dad ten years ago, there were countless times that those who knew him described him as a man with incredible integrity. I often wondered what the circumstances were and how they knew him. It gave me pause for thought on many occasions, and still does, to think how people will describe me when I am gone, and would integrity be something they say about me.

In the book, "A Fathers Legacy" left for my sister and I, were the handwritten words of a man who wanted his daughters to know his heart and final thoughts on life. While going through chemotherapy or blood transfusions he would sit and handwrite word-for-word his nuggets of wisdom that would be a legacy after he was gone. I think daily on these words and though I know I cannot go back and rewrite some of the decisions I made when I did not place integrity first in my life choices or path, I use this as a compass and know that he would be proud of me.

> "Maintain absolute integrity. Don't initiate or participate in anything that contravenes your personal values. No price is worth the loss of integrity."
> Tom McRae March 28, 1964 – June 1, 2004

Following a provincial competition, which I won, I was quickly absorbed into the life that comes with it. Clothing lines and supplement companies were knocking at my door; I was writing for online magazines and sharing my story on social media at a rapid pace. It wasn't long after this that I was scouted for a well-known fitness modeling competition, and despite my hesitation at first, the opportunity was incredible and I stepped into this also.

The above quote and integrity principle that I attributed to my life up until that point was slipping through my fingers. Was I participating in a way that contravened my personal values? Yes. Did I feel good about it? No I didn't, but I liked the attention and it filled a void I had in years past during my time of obesity and depression. So despite my best attempts to say I would be careful and not get swept up into the industry or do whatever it took to get to the top, I saw it happening before my own eyes.

The truth is, I love the stage and I loved the people who I met, and what I was able to accomplish. What I didn't love was that I sacrificed my health and my family in order to get to the stage. I didn't do it with the integrity principles that are integral to my life.

Do I still love health and fitness, modeling and being a proud representative in this industry? Absolutely! Every experience is a lesson and an opportunity to gain more wisdom, and so this nugget of wisdom I leave you with is one from my life that I have learned recently.

Integrity in our life must be the compass that allows us to know when we step into something, step back out, or watch from the sidelines. I have happily spent some time watching from the sidelines and reprioritizing my life. In doing so, these actions have me stronger, healthier and feeling more whole than ever before.

Nugget Two: Respect is Given, not Earned

The second nugget of wisdom is the value I place on respect being given and not earned. This might not resonate with everyone reading this and may even take a moment of head scratching to wrap your head around. It may even seem contrary, in fact, to today's standard of getting to the top first or the idea you must do something in order to receive something in return.

However, how many times in life do we hear the phrase or term, "respect is earned"? I've found that frequently it's said by an authority figure or in a way to elicit a response or call to action. I know that when I hear people say, "respect is earned," one person typically has less power or position than the other.

The reason I have a challenging time with this and believe that respect must be given as opposed to earned is that my core belief system says that all people are equal and that all people have not experienced respect in their lives.

My experiences with Aboriginal persons, youth at risk, and women in crisis over the last twenty years has shown me that most of these individuals and groups of people have had very little respect given to them in their early years. As such, it's been hard for me over the years to see youth and adult clients struggle and be labeled as confrontational, belligerent, and unwilling.

Ultimately, throughout my career there have been countless lessons my clients have taught me, which has influenced who I am and how I live my life. Ironically, their vulnerability and constant state of crisis were parallels for the stability, integrity, and character I found in the lessons my dad left for me.

Through my own life experiences, I have found camaraderie with those who don't fit into society norms. I believe it is because I have demonstrated respect to others for their gifts and abilities, and who they are as individuals that I am the coach, speaker, and entrepreneur I am today.

I believe that because I respected them as individuals and showed that I was no better than they were that they learned respect and this naturally flowed. This way of living and treating others is how I embrace life.

Nugget Three: Follow Your Heart

I had not understood the true meaning of following your heart until this year. I have experienced following my heart for love or natural experiences, but never for stepping out and taking a risk beyond reason or logic.

The kind that when you share your idea, others shake their head and ask questions that make you feel small, as the facts are stacked up against you. All these were true for me as I began to vocalize the idea of putting on a high end Gala for women in need in only six weeks' time at Christmas. I believe that sometimes the greatest ideas come to us when we are doing the most mundane of tasks because our heart and mind is open to receive, and it's our gifts and abilities that can be aligned to this receiving.

And so it was while I was vacuuming and thinking about all the advertisements for upcoming Christmas events, parties, and the costs associated with them. All across the media were announcements for women to come and get their nails, hair, and outfits done at one salon or another, pick out their dress for Christmas or the New Year's party they were attending. It was in these moments I couldn't help but think about those who would never make it into the salon for a hair appointment or the clothing store for a new dress. The thought of a seventy-five dollar party ticket was certainly out of my range this Christmas and had been over the years as a single mom, and even at times while married and we both worked double jobs to try and make ends meet.

Following my heart and investing every hour I could for six weeks meant that we were able to reach 225 women and provide them with full salon services, clothing, shoes, and accessories to wear at the Gala that evening and more. In the evening, we turned the dull and dreary non-profit mission into a winter wonderland for the women to bring their children in for childcare while they enjoyed a rich, classy, and elegant evening with one another in an adjacent room. The most expressed testimonials from the women were that each woman felt respected, honored, and valued during the day and evening by the volunteers. This was not an event focusing on outreach, a specific program need, trying to raise money, or talk about their needs and pressing issues. My heart was to truly celebrate *all* women, bring them together in one place, and demonstrate their worth and value through our service and compassion.

Despite not having any money or volunteers, I had an idea and I followed my heart, which led to the success of ten teams, over eighty volunteers, and all the funds we needed to now lead us into the development of a Charity Events organization to provide women in need with the much deserved celebrations they have been without.

Following your heart may get you some funny looks and doors slammed in your face, especially when you are dealing with the economic business world. This will likely be the case if you are a visionary with a creative mind. Never let your ideas go unheard because ideas are what keep this world moving forward. If I had never voiced my idea and shared my heart, this Gala would never have happened. These women ultimately would never have come.

Follow your heart.

Gillian FAITH

Gillian Faith

Gillian Faith is a professional speaker, lifestyle coach, and social entrepreneur. She is committed to using a holistic and comprehensive approach to increase the quality of life, satisfaction, and success of her audience. She offers a large scale of speaking services at major events, intimate customized workshops for individual organizations, and personalized consulting services.

Utilizing her twenty-year background in community development and social work, she is well aware of the ongoing issues and needs of citizens within the marginalized community. Gillian has competed previously in multiple athletic events, and was crowned "BC's Strongest Woman" in 2013. She was scouted for the Fitness Star International Model Search by James K. Erdt at the 2013 Canfitpro event in Vancouver and competed in August. Perhaps her most notable accomplishment, however, would be the loss of over one hundred pounds during her own personal transformative process following the loss of her father and her divorce.

She is a proud mother of three children and is happily remarried and living in Kamloops, BC. She is a guiding light to those around her. Anyone in direct contact with her is provided an immediate opportunity for growth through supported self-reflection, inspiration, and motivation. For more information, please visit Gillian's website at www.gilliansfaith.com or connect with her at connect@gilliansfaith.com

If You're Looking for a Sign, This is it!

By Gina Hatzis

Define and Re-define Success for Yourself

I had just landed a position in the newsroom at CityTV, a popular station in downtown Toronto. At home we celebrated as if I had won an Academy Award—special dinner and champagne…after all, I had arrived!

So four months in, when I drafted my letter of resignation and quit my job, I had to use smelling salts to revive my mother.

If I am honest with myself, I can say I knew right away that journalism was not for me. I felt like the Grim Reaper—gathering the worst news of the day and disseminating the dire state of the world upon the masses. Dramatic perhaps, but I definitely knew it was not the energy I wanted to put out there.

My well-intentioned friends and family told me I was nuts throwing away the opportunity of a lifetime. As a life-long people pleaser, I was tormented by everyone's opinions and lack of faith in my decision. I was also young and disillusioned about success and how to go about "getting it," so I did the unthinkable.

I put my tail between my legs and begged for my job back.

And unbelievably—unfortunately—I got it.

Then the real torment began because I now had to prove I was worthy of a second chance. I probably should have won an Academy Award for my performance. I mustered up the façade of enthusiasm and dedication. I even mastered the smooth on-camera transition from "Thirty-four people have died in a train wreck, heart disease in children under twelve is on the rise and a sexual predator may be loose in your neighbourhood" to "Let's take a look at today's Lotto numbers!"—and cut!

My redemption barely lasted a few months.

I got a job in the collections department of a call centre, biding my time until I could figure out next steps. I accepted my Grim Reaper's karma and spent my summer in a two-by-two cubicle, tethered to a desk, reciting a script that ensured I maintained superior customer relations and a call length of less than ninety seconds.

Yup, rock bottom.

I poured myself into self-help books, obsessed with discovering my life's purpose. Although I wasn't exactly clear on what I wanted, I knew what I didn't want.

So, when I stumbled across the opportunity to become a magician, dangling promises of a flexible schedule, higher hourly rate and the chance to bring joy into people's lives, I jumped on it quicker than you can say abracadabra.

I was happier than I had been in a long time; while acutely aware I hadn't yet found my "thing." My friends noticed the change in me and asked me what I had learned. I put together a booklet about finding your passion and invited a group of friends to meet in my basement once a month. There was no fee, and yet the payoff was a yummy potluck, meaningful conversation—oh, and a light bulb.

The light bulb over my head lit up after my first session when I realized that by helping others find their purpose, I had found mine.

I initially registered my business as *Project Passion* with the sole purpose of honing my craft as a facilitator and optimistically breaking even. Within three months, I was offered one thousand dollars to speak to a group of bank managers. In less than a year, I was working regularly as a speaker and trainer. Twenty years, one marriage and two children later, I am living an entrepreneurial life that I could not have crafted in my wildest dreams.

But here's the dig: I never felt successful.

Success meant unlimited affluence, employees to pay, and an interview with Oprah Winfrey. Reading business books and attending seminars to "Boost Profits and Expand Your Customer Base" only illuminated the snail-paced growth of Project Passion. After fifteen years, shouldn't I be further along? And why wasn't Oprah calling?

So I began researching success. What was it? How do I get it? What was I doing wrong?

I didn't find the answer in a book, on the Internet, or by speaking to successful people. I found the answer by reviewing my life.

For me, success is a path lined with a set of flags, each bringing me closer to my personal entrepreneurial nirvana. The first flag of success meant quitting my television job and trusting my gut. The second was breaking away from the "nine to five" mindset to craft a life where I could create my own schedule and also share something meaningful with the world.

Subsequent flags included a business plan that allowed me the financial freedom to start a family, be home to raise my children through their formative years, and schedule my days around dentist appointments and yoga classes. Today, I have stretched my definition of success to include putting energy into the world that aligns my gifts with bringing light and hope to others. And the path continues.

The very first step to success, business or otherwise, is taking the time to define and re-define it for yourself, based on what is important to you.

It takes time. It takes grit. It takes honesty and introspection. It takes a double dose of courage and triple scoop of faith. Mix it all together and we find our days filled with meaning and fuelled by a spectrum of success markers that are both attainable and rewarding. In this way, we are no longer striving for a finish line that continues to blur and elude us like a mirage in the desert. When my definition of success is clearly defined by me, I am empowered to decide day by day if I'm on the right track.

Profits and growth are not the only yardsticks to measure the success of business. My personal yardsticks include how amazing I feel on Monday mornings while the rest of the world moans and groans, the spontaneity of a mid-day walk in nature, volunteering at my kids' school, the opportunity to stretch myself every day to create meaningful content, receiving a raving testimonial from a client, or the thrill of speaking to a roomful of soul-seekers.

Woven into the fabric of the entrepreneurial mindset is this toxic belief that bigger is better, profit is power, and sales are supreme. I bought into this belief years ago, and I'm looking for a refund. As a woman entrepreneur in the twenty-first century, I stand for a radically new definition of success—one that encompasses and honors all of the roles I play. It is my responsibility and my privilege to craft my personal definition of success. And it is yours.

> *"Today you are You, that is truer than true.*
> *There is no one alive who is You-er than You."*
> —Dr. Seuss

I don't come from a family of entrepreneurs. My posse tends to shoot for the twenty-five-year gold watch and fringe benefits. So I have always been hungry for a mentor—someone to show me the way, to make it easy for me, basically to save me. I'm pretty sure this is called the Prince Charming Syndrome.

And yet, I fantasized about an older female sage, oddly cloaked in a white toga, infusing me with her knowledge and guiding me to make smart business decisions (while a harp plays softly in the background). When she didn't arrive, I latched onto the coattails of the first successful entrepreneur I could find. My guru took the form of a charismatic twenty-nine-year-old businessman named Philip Murad.

Philip was a big thinker, a risk-taker, a marketing maverick, and I admired the way his brain worked—probably because it was so different from mine. I watched him closely, taking mental notes as his business grew exponentially, and thinking to myself, "I'll just replicate whatever he's doing." I slowly became aware of the great divide between his business approach, unique talents, and my own—realizing that I would have to forge my own path.

Over the years, I have met many entrepreneurs. I have read their books, participated in their seminars, and picked their brains. I have gained tremendous value in their wisdom, especially in areas that I know little about. I am a lover of learning, so more was always better—more opinions, more approaches, more guidance. The voices in my head got so loud that I soon couldn't hear my own and often lost touch with the essence of my gift. And after years of trying to squeeze myself into their well-worn jeans, here is what I know for sure.

I cannot be successful by being anything but authentically me.

Sure I can adopt marketing strategies and get advice on website design from the people who know, and I can certainly gain inspiration from the gurus I study and admire.

And yet, when I look at where in my business I am most impactful, most valuable to my audience, most energized, most profitable—it is undeniably when I am most "Gina."

A mentor can show you a way—their way to success. But it's only their way, not the only way. We mustn't be afraid to blaze our own trails and go off-road a little while doing so; trusting our inner GPS to bring us home to a place we recognize.

I have been paralyzed and intimidated by the thought of all the competition out there and of all the ways I could be better. While there may be many people out there doing what I do, there is no one doing it the way I do it. And the same is true for you. Never underestimate the value of your unique fingerprint on the world.

After all, no one could be You-er than You!

Timing is not everything.

Oprah Winfrey was looking straight at me. Her mouth was moving and I'm pretty sure words were coming out. All I heard was Charlie Brown's teacher, "Wah, wah, wah." She was answering a question I can't even remember asking. A question about timing. "How do you know when it's time to pursue your dream? When can you trust the time is right?"

It was definitely an out-of-body moment. I was at a taping of an Oprah Winfrey show called "What Do I Want to Do with My Life," showcasing entrepreneurs who successfully pursued their passion. Synchronicity was flaunting her impeccable sense of timing because I was at a definite, post-graduate crossroads. On the one hand, I had an impossible dream that ached to be realized. On the other, I didn't have the experience, know-how, or the audacity to believe I could make it happen.

The audience was thrilled to be gifted with free mink slippers and red velvet cupcakes, but I was tormented by the notion of timing.

I didn't even hear Oprah's response to my question until I got home and reviewed the VHS tape.

"Perfect time? There's no such thing. Now is the time. Don't wait for the perfect moment—it will never come. Go now. Begin. Today."

This would be a great story if I told you that my life changed in that moment; that I mustered the faith and courage to chase my dream because "Oprah said so." Sorry to disappoint. It seemed I lost my confidence on the flight home from Chicago to Toronto. And although I did slowly, eventually pursue my dream, it took me a decade to really internalize what she meant.

There are a million reasons not to start now: the economy, personal finances, time restraints, familial responsibilities, lack of resources, discomfort, and my thighs.

There is only one reason to start now: now is the only moment we have.

When I get weak at the knees and my reptilian brain urges me to flee, I remind myself that I don't need to know the next twenty steps—only the next step. I dig deep—past the naysayers, the media, the critics, the well-meaning advice, and finally past my comfort zone into the deepest part of myself.

I get quiet and tune into my inner wisdom that softly whispers, "Now."

Although the road is not always straight or clear, I know that any steps, even small ones, even wrong ones, move me forward. When the fear and doubt creep up, put your hand on your heart. That thump, thump, thump is the ticking hands of time reminding you of its flight, which none can stop and that money cannot buy.

And now for your homework assignment.

Write yourself a letter from your eighty-five-year-old self. What words of wisdom would you share? What regrets might you have?

Words unspoken?

Missed opportunities? Time wasted?

Now is the time. Start small. Start anywhere. But start.

And if you are waiting for a sign…This is it.

Gina Hatzis

Gina is the Founder and Director of *Possibilities at Project Passion International* where she helps people transform all areas of their lives by transforming their relationship with themselves.

For the past two decades Gina has been committed to inspiring people out of their mediocrity into lives of purpose and meaning. Her audiences span every corporate level from C-Suite to front line employee, in a multitude of industries from telecom to insurance, retail to industrial, hospitality to media. She also joyfully offers workshops to empower women, especially moms, to ignite self-love, and offers insights to grade eight students about the power of choice.

She is a big believer in the power of living consciously. Her philosophy is encompassed in personal accountability—being individually responsible for positive outcomes at work and home, by adopting small shifts in thought, intention, and action.

For more information, please visit Gina's website at www.ginahatzis.com www.facebook.com/projectpassioninternational

Wake the Flipper Up
The Simple Formula To Unlocking Your Purpose

By Giuditta Gareri

A little of my background. I was raised by an Italian immigrant entrepreneurial family that held the mentality: "You have to work hard to survive." Life was all about work and no play. As a young woman in a male dominant aggressive industry, the world of real estate, my family owned the #1 RE/MAX brokerage that housed mainly top producers. I was surrounded by entrepreneurs who earned no less than $100k per year, some over 1-2 million dollars, and everything in between. This was my world; I didn't know anything else existed.

I completed my real estate licensing at sixteen, completed my broker's license at seventeen, and was legally licensed at eighteen. The goal: complete all licensing before university. I was working seven days a week, carrying a twenty-four hour pager, and managing staff. In my early twenties, I was managing and recruiting top sales representatives while running a large organization. At twenty-six, I took the next logical step outside of my family business and joined the top coaching and training company for real estate salespeople in Canada. I was coaching, training, and speaking to thousands of realtors on how to reach higher levels of success. The youngest professional coach in the industry, I was always striving for the next level. Looking at my life you would think I had it all—a high powered career through which I could get anything I wanted.

Yet somewhere deep inside I wasn't happy but couldn't understand why.

The 24/7 mentality led me to many challenges and struggles with internal battles and addictions. I experienced everything from overspending, chasing the high lifestyle, smoking, alcohol, binge eating, love and drama. I also experienced the emotional highs and lows, which included major depressions that eventually lead to a serious major crash and burn. Even worse, between the ages of twenty-five and twenty-six my life spiraled downward as I struggled to cope with the losing the love of my life to cancer: my beloved father. I stood by his side and watched his slow, debilitating slide towards death until the very end.

My world as I once knew it shattered. I began to question everything. Why was I doing what I was doing? Where is my life going? How can I ever put my life together again? With my "rock" gone, I struggled to find stable ground. My health suffered, as did my financial well-being, my long-term relationship, the safety net which was my family business—my mother chose to sell to retire herself—my future, my retirement: my entire identity was threatened! All of these things defined me; who was I without any of them? I reached a point of physical, emotional and financial devastation. I found myself having to rebuild my entire life from scratch, from nothing, all over again after all those years of hard work.

I asked myself what I truly wanted this time around. I wanted to choose my future and design it with precision and care. I wasn't going to do anything or live in a way to impress anyone or to gain acceptance. I wanted to live my life the way I wanted to, on my own terms, and to experience life on purpose. As I reflected back on my life, a realization struck me. Through all of my success and challenges, and through the people I worked with, I began to see the qualities of those who were actually happy and had **sustainable** success.

I also learned so much about those who seemed to constantly struggle emotionally, financially and/or physically. I came to realize that deep down everyone wanted to know the secret to having success, to happiness, to living on purpose, and to fulfillment. This time I was determined to get it right.

My father, one of my greatest inspirations in life, was always a happy person. It broke his heart to watch his daughter so unhappy in life and not being able to do anything about it. When he was sick and knew his time was near, he asked me to promise that I would commit the rest of my life to becoming happy. Once I learned what happiness was for me, I was to share what I have learned with others. My father told me that this would allow me to continue to keep the newfound happiness for myself. After I made that promise, I intended to do anything and everything in my power to keep it.

From that day forward I have been on a serious mission to figure out a simple formula for happiness. And once I figured it out for myself, I would commit to sharing this with others. Now you know why I wrote this chapter, and why I'm sharing with you today. I am fulfilling that sacred promise I made to my father. I pursued my mission using the same drive I applied to the first twenty-six years of my life. Over the past decade, I've been searching to discover the formula that would bring true peace and fulfillment.

Now, before continuing to read, I want you to first ask yourself, "Am I sure I want to know the secret to finding out your purpose and mission in this lifetime?" Let me ask you, "Are you sure you want to know the formula on how to discover your purpose, how to be happy, and how to create any result you desire in any area of your life?" Be sure of your reply, because once you know the answer to this question there's NO going back. You will have two choices: you either have to IGNORE it and KNOW that you're ignoring it. Or it will be time to take responsibility for making anything and everything happen in your life. You will no longer be able to point fingers outside of yourself, say that its someone else's fault that your life is the way it is, or that it's because of this or that circumstance. Your happiness, your results, and your fulfillment in life will be completely in *your own hands* from this moment forward. So be sure ... be really sure that you want to know.

Okay, here goes ...

It begins with a concept called **LEADERSHIP**. True happiness begins as a result of being a LEADER in your own life. Leadership equates to results, to success, to love, money or career, family friends, health—all of it. You must be willing and able to *lead yourself* first before you will be able to successfully lead others to success.

The Formula:

DISCOVER + DEVELOP + DELIVER = PURPOSE / MISSION
Your Unique Gifts & Talents   Happiness & Fulfillment

When you take leadership of your life, you can work through the formula, which can be simplified into the 3 D's: Discover, Develop and Deliver your unique and special talents to the world. This is where the magic comes in. It's where everything happens, and it's a lifelong process. It leads us to discovering our PURPOSE for our life, and what and why we are here. **Our purpose is to actually discover, develop and deliver our unique God-given talents to the world! Only then can we experience happiness.** It really is that simple.

Discover

First we have to **Discover** who we are, what we're good at, what we're not so good at, and come to terms with and **accept** these things. Discovering our strengths and weaknesses is the process of **self-discovery**. Once you're able to know everything you are, everything you're not, and everything you *never* will be—and you are able to come to terms with these—then you've reached self-acceptance, which equates to self-confidence.

As Discovery happens, power, clarity and energy shine through everything you do. *It's when who you are, what you say, and what you do are in total alignment.* Look and see; there may be areas in your life that you have this power and clarity naturally, and other areas that you don't.

Developing mastery of the SELF is leadership. It takes introspection, responsibility and courage to look at ourselves to see what's missing or could be improved. Leaders face things. They don't throw anything under the rug. They face the **truth**, the reality of themselves and of life, and go head first into all of it; they know on the other side of facing everything is the power and opportunity to make a difference in the world.

As we grow and develop through discovery of our own unique talents and passions, we can then commit to **developing** these talents and abilities throughout our lives. We are truly committed to our own growth and to taking responsibility for the gifts and talents we were given and born with. We make a **LIFELONG commitment** to developing our gifts & talents. This means practice, practice, practice, until the discoveries we made lead us to MASTERY. This is a lifelong process; there's always more to discover, to learn, to practice.

Mastery of your unique gifts and talents is not a destination, it's more of a process that you should enjoy because when you are focused on developing your natural talents and abilities, time just flows and problems melt away. You're in the here and now, the present. You're in the zone, and that's all you want and are searching for—to experience these moments of bliss.

As you can see, in the process lies the gift that we've been searching for which leads us to our Purpose.

Deliver

The next level is to **Deliver** our gifts and talents to the world. Once we discover and develop them, there comes a point where we can no longer keep them to ourselves. If we do, we will notice a stagnation in our lives, a dissatisfaction. Something begins to nag at us deep inside. We feel bored, we may turn to eating, drugs, alcohol, TV, social media, shopping or other distractions to avoid this feeling. The truth is, we try to avoid taking responsibility for what's nagging at us deep within. Here we are born with these amazing unique gifts and talents that the world needs, the reason we were created, and we're hoarding them! This dissatisfaction comes from having these gifts and NOT SHARING them with the world in some way. They are called "gifts" for a reason: they're meant to be given away!! It's our responsibility to share our gifts, in doing so we receive the special gift we've always wanted: *we get to experience fulfillment, passion and happiness*—in everything we were meant to experience.

How can we DELIVER our talents? The ways are endless. An artist will create and share art, writers will share their thoughts and ideas, doctors help others in need, speakers get their message to more people, some volunteer for causes, some will do it within their careers. The way in which we want to express our gifts and talents to the world doesn't matter, we just have to find our own unique way to express them. Nurse by day, singer by night; teacher and dance performer; bartender and comedian. The gifts, talents and passions or expressions of each are ENDLESS. *It's our mission and purpose to Discover and develop them, as we develop them we must simultaneously DELIVER them to the world. That's the secret formula to achieve your purpose and fulfill your desires.*

The trouble is that people seem get stuck at the beginning. We're in a world where we're told what is "normal, how to be, and what to be like". By the time we're ready to fulfill our purpose, we're buried by expectations and the status quo. There are so many factors stifling our creativity, trying to make us all the same, which is crazy! We're all created differently for a REASON. Expression of our unique individuality is what transforms the world and makes a difference; it's what is required to move this world powerfully forward. Once you truly get this and remove these layers during your self discovery phase, you're on your way to breaking through to the next level in your life and beyond—towards True Freedom!

Now you have it: the formula to success, happiness and fulfillment. Those who put this formula into play have found their groove and are living on purpose each and every single day … and now so can you!

Until next time,

"Life is Short. Live Your Dreams & Share Your Passions."

—G

Giuditta Gareri

Giuditta was literally born into the real estate industry beside hundreds of six and seven figure income earners. The family business became one of the top producing REMAX organizations in Canada. Guiditta went on to coach, train and develop leaders in her industry across North America. Through these experiences, she has built a powerful worldview of entrepreneurship, which has shaped her personal and professional life.

Guiditta was licensed at the age of eighteen and a broker by twenty, but don't let her youth fool you. She is a wise soul, and a lifetime surrounded by entrepreneurs gives her the ability to share an incredible inside view on how to build a highly successful business and become a powerful leader. With her vast experience in selling, running teams, managing, recruiting, training, and coaching, Guiditta is a powerhouse of entrepreneurial and leadership knowledge through real life experience.

Giuditta's philosophy, in life and business, is full of grace. She believes that we were all born with unique gifts and talents. Our mission and purpose in this life in this lifetime are simple: in this lifetime are simple: to relentlessly take the time to discover, develop, and deliver these unique gifts and talents in service of a better world. She states that success, balance, peace, power, abundance, and fulfillment are found in the discovery of our unique purpose and mission. Doing what we love, loving what we do, naturally and effectively fulfilling what we are most passionate about: this builds a successful business and life.

www.giudittagareri.com

Spiritual Warrior

∞

By Ilina Ivana AstroCoach #ONELOVE

There was a time when Cinderella thought that the world was made of a sparkling glitter until the stepmother convinced her otherwise. Hello beautiful people. How does it feel to get stuck within your own talent and be unable to breathe? How does it feel to be blessed with great wisdom, knowledge, and spiritual intelligence, but yet not be able to soar? How does it feel to know that there is more to life other than mere existence?

I can vividly remember the day when I said to my mother how much I wanted to go to India and how I literary threw a tantrum when she thought that I was totally crazy for listening to too much adult talk and gossip. The truth was that my mother was oblivious to my talents and didn't acknowledge the past life experiences I'd had as a three-year-old child. I had absolutely no idea at that time what India was or what it represented. These events continued to escalate as I grew up, but I have remained myself, unique, rebellious, and hungry for knowledge. When I was five or six years old, I had a good idea about God, Jesus, and supernatural entities. I would constantly see shimmering lights, sparkles, and little stars shining above my head. Well, that didn't work so well with my mom since she always suspected that I needed a psychologist. That kind of restriction from my parents caused my rebellious streak to grow greater and out of proportion. I was a troubled teen in the eyes of my parents, especially when I decided to become a teen mom and quit schooling. It was a shock to my whole family. I graduated from school at a later date, but chose to ensure my son was raised well and would have all opportunities in life. He was my safe haven. When I got pregnant, my clairvoyance was born, and this is when I heard for the first time that I had to keep my baby regardless of the consequences.

The increasing desire for me to learn and read about spirituality, occult (yes I have read everything imaginable), philosophy, religions of the world, and so forth was strong. It grew more profoundly as I was getting into my early teens, and that is exactly when I started to channel my first intuitive messages. Being born in Serbia (former Yugoslavia) and raised on many superstitious beliefs, which originate from the Osman Empire, reading the Turkish coffee cup was a nationwide habit, and in my case a true talent. I remember during the hot summer vacations sitting under my grandmother's big porch covered with an abundance of vine leaves in the southern region of Serbia and reading our neighbor's cups of delicious yet unbearably strong, Turkish coffee. They were always in awe of me after these readings and once I had shed some light on their life affairs.

Life for me was not always about living my passion and giving messages of hope to others. I had to fight for that which I believed to be my birthright, and to be happy and content. I remember children bullying me during elementary school because I was a "witch," a newcomer (my mother forced me to change schools after we moved even though it wasn't necessary), an outsider, and other such non-endearing terms. Somehow, my peers and even the teachers presumed that it was ok to pick on me, to bully me, put me down, or even to punish me. All this without good reason. Their goal, known to themselves or not, was simply to cultivate ignorance and fear inside their own souls instead of accepting me as beautiful, vulnerable, knowledgeable, and blessed with something much more different than their vision of the world. The idea of uniqueness was lost on them, and so was I.

I was innately blessed—despite being born in a communist country—to have had an opportunity to travel the world and live in several different countries, meet some extraordinary souls that I call friends today, and experience many good things along the way. And all while dealing with the perplexities of life, and of course, discovering my own uniqueness and driving core, which illuminated my path to this very day.

During those years I had nothing but difficulties when it came to expressing my true self and my true gifts. I had suppressed my divine right of self-expression that we all possess and instead went with the monotony of daily routine, to make ends meet. Those were my dark years because I lived in the debris of my own shadow, unable to express how I truly felt, handicapped in my inability to stand up for my true self like I did in my younger years. I was totally oblivious to my tremendous inner power; the power of a ONELOVE WARRIOR. While I am typing this, tears are rolling uncontrollably down my cheeks because I remember how dead I felt in my soul. I was destitute because my resentment was overruling everything. I had to endure constant judgment and impolite scrutiny from everyone in my life.

Eventually, and luckily for me, something extraordinary and life-liberating happened—I fell in love! Meeting the love of my life, Luciano, opened the door to glorious Canada and suddenly added a new meaning to my life, a new purpose. Slowly my buried talents were resurrected. Just the simple feeling of being loved was the boost my super-charged soul and immense storage of intuition needed to start flowing again. My divinity guides took me back to the old and familiar world of innate gifts, my birthright, and my legacy. The ONELOVE WARRIOR within me was reborn!

Shortly after moving to "O Canada our home and native land" I went back to studying my beloved Astrology. I needed to define the meaning of how to use my gifts properly, because let's face it, who would want to be a reader of the Turkish coffee cup for the rest of their life? I know this may sound tedious, but truly, why would I want my gifts to go unnoticed? How could I possibly give people better guidance unless I could reach out to them through something powerful like Astrology?

I finally found my niche, my power source, my revelation, and my ultimate spiritual tool—Astrology: the oldest form of prophecy in human history. Did you know that Astrology is actually an ancient science that predates both astronomy and psychology? Astrology is the mother of all wisdoms and the glorified science of the planetary influence!

SPIRITUAL WARRIOR had risen from the ashes. My higher conscious mind had finally embodied my earthbound body. When I did my first reading I felt the immense strength and serenity, and the intensity was equal as the moment of giving birth to my handsome son, Vlad. I could hear my guides and my angels whispering to me: "You are finally here; you've arrived to your safe haven." No more hiding in the spiritual closet. No more insecurities. The true *me* had emerged radiant and victorious.

This story is a true breakthrough, you are probably thinking while you're reading this. Not so quickly my beautiful friends, the story has just begun followed by its first challenge. The whole purpose of having a divine gift is to utilize it to its fullest capabilities; otherwise it becomes just an idle talent you used to have. This made me question myself. Do I just want to give people predictions or the rundown on the following years in their lives? Would I like to give them more than just one piece of the puzzle? I truly believed in myself and my capabilities and I believed they were more than just about foreseeing future events.

Helping others is my religion, my God of wisdom and my Goddess of guidance. What kind of a ONELOVE WARRIOR would I be if I couldn't find the way to help guide others so they could feel the same way I do, empowered and revived? How could I hide that light inside me? Is my talent really a talent if I don't share it with others? How could I encapsulate the feeling of hope and compassion if not by spreading my wisdom of intuition and spiritual guidance onto others so they could learn to soar and live in the beauty of their own enriched soul?

I have met many exceptional people in my life, ranging from highly educated, gifted, ambitious, and yet also highly sensitive, emotionally rich, spiritually rich, capable beyond this earthy realm and beyond their years. Old and wise souls, my divine brothers and sisters. One thing they all had in common was they all had to undertake life transitions and challenges and overcome them. We must all go through extensive ordeals and perplexities in our daily existence. It is a part of life and a part of the way.

It took many years of struggle and tough earthy existence for me to learn to let bygones be bygones, to accept my sparkling being for what it really is and to eliminate the resentment. I am against any form of judgment for that reason; I simply can't tolerate the fact that we are sometimes deeply imbedded in the feeling of shame, guilt, or taboo, thereby developing judgment or negativity that we later project onto our loved ones, peers, friends, and eventually the world around us. It weakens us tremendously, strips our soul to its bare minimum until we undermine our own well-being and give up on hope. This is when I made a pact with myself, God, my spirit guides and angels. The direction that I am striding today is called ONELOVE and ONENESS; freedom of spirit, freedom of self-expression, freedom of wonderful YOU, and fabulous ME! My clients often ask me, "What are the correct ways to deal with inner struggles or inner hurts?"

My answer is simple, "Happiness is attainable in large quantities for everyone involved!" The moment you discard the anger, bitterness, or self-scrutiny and take a direction called ONELOVE, you will embark on your final road to a happier and healthier YOU!

You don't need other people's approval; you just need your own approval. You've been through so many refractory situations in your life, whether you choose to admit it or not, and that sacrifice and hardship elevated you to the highest realm of becoming a real survivor and a warrior of light.

Do you think that others will love you more? Have you ever given yourself praise for all your scars and emotional wounds? Do you think that the sun is born at every dawn without the help of the sparkling stars and the moon? The answer is tattooed in your heart; therefore, why wouldn't you love yourself and accept your divine existence? We learn love from loving our inner God or Goddess first. My greatest lesson in life was exactly that affirmation, the affirmation that "I choose to love and accept myself." I choose to attract what nourishes my soul, what makes my heart sing, and what helps me embrace what I really want and who I really want to become.

Life is all about you soaring and thriving. Make no mistake, if you think that your life is worthless or not significant enough to serve the purpose, it will become as such. In case you do have that core belief, you better wake up from the nightmare called needing approval from others. Core beliefs that you should infinitely embrace are:

1. Love yourself and every living thing
2. Value yourself and others
3. Uniqueness is your birthright
4. Never lose your inner child
5. Believe in miracles because you are one!

My dear ONELOVEWARRIORS, remember that your definition of acceptance will influence your levels of happiness.

My greatest intention is to change the world by doing one spiritual reading at a time. My spiritual advising is based on the following philosophy: If you show people how to get in touch with their true divine light that comes from within, you can illuminate their whole life and make it extraordinary.

Yours truly Ilina Ivana AstroCoach #ONELOVE

Ilina Ivana Astrocoach
"Clarivoyant For The Stars!"

Ilina Ivana is a Professional Astrologer/Intuitive & Spiritual Advisor specializing in helping people by uniting her true passion for the purpose of assisting others in mind, body and spirit. She has extensive experience in the field of Astrology, Spiritual doctrines and she has developed her unique style and way of working with clients. Her specialty is Spiritual readings, Channelled messages, Emotional Healing and providing others with insightful advice. Ilina Ivana's ongoing dedication is to inspire others to connect with their truth and higher self. Ilina Ivana established her private practice in Europe in early 90's and continued to gain practical experience with exceptional results in Toronto, Canada since 2007. "Master your destiny and reach for the stars!"

www.astrocoach.ca
info@astrocoach.ca
www.facebook.com/astrocoach4u
Office: 647-342-2077

Pure Success

By James MacNeil

Congratulations on deciding to acquire this book and congratulations for opening the pages and reading what you're reading now. I know it's very rare for someone to make an investment in personal development rather than in entertainment today. You, however, have invested in yourself, in your future, in your ability to impact your family, your friends, your finances, and the world that you touch. Once again, congratulations!

This book is a compilation of success ideas, insights, principles, processes, strategies, and stories. It's a buffet of great ideas from great people. I suggest that you take it all in, without judgment. Gather it all up and put it all in your intellectual hopper. After you're done, make the decisions of what you want to use, refuse, and store for future use.

When I'm asked how I "made it," I give a variety of answers. Herein you will receive my best possible, and purest answer. My journey started with a challenging childhood wherein I struggled greatly with Attention Deficit and Hyperactivity Disorder (ADHD). I found it virtually impossible to connect and communicate with anyone. I found myself feeling alone, lost, and unloved. I felt as if I couldn't trust anyone; that life was cruel and unforgiving and I was convinced I lacked the basic ingredients to "make it." I found myself at the age of nineteen functionally illiterate and in a suicidal depression in Fort Lauderdale, Florida, without any degrees, inheritance, or hope. Today I've been blessed with an amazing career and I'm one of the highest paid corporate consultants, national best-selling authors, and international motivational speakers. In the last fifteen months I've circled the globe four times sharing the stage with Les Brown, Steve Forbes, Tom Hopkins, Larry King, Rudy Giuliani, Tony Buzan, Mary Buffett, Robert Allen, Chris Gardner and Sir Richard Branson. I've also shared the stage with, and/or worked with, Harv Eker, Bob Proctor, Mark Victor Hanson and Anthony Robbins. How did all that happen? I give all the glory to God for His blessings. I know that answer will annoy many people, so let me expand my answer to include what I think I've done right and, therefore, what I suggest for your serious consideration.

Pure Ambition

I'm genuinely motivated to always look for the best conceivable outcome. I want to be the best possible version of myself. I want to live my best possible life. No matter what I put my hand to, I want to be the best I possibly can be.

I've noticed that drive, motivation, ambition, or whatever you call it, is essential for progress and accomplishment. As Denis Waitley has stated, "You are habitually focused on either 'tension relieving' or 'goal achieving.'" We are naturally compelled to Live, Love, Learn, and Leave a Legacy so it doesn't matter how "easy" or "tough" your journey has been thus far. What matters is whether you've utilized your experience to stoke these fires of motivation and drive.

For me, it began with a desperate quest for attention and approval. Maybe that came from my childhood longing for love, approval, and attention from my father. He was a good man, and a good father in many ways, but I felt that I was not loved as much as my siblings were and definitely not loved as much as I felt I needed to be. I strove to get that attention and that approval through performance, specifically through scoring goals in hockey. That performance habit continued into my work life. I strove to be the very best I could be, to stretch, grow, learn, perform, achieve, and impress.

My original motivations may seem adolescent, but that's because they were. I developed a motivational habit, but my ambitions needed to mature. We can be motivated for a season by the "lack" of basic human needs, but what happens when these needs are met? Abraham Maslow's *Hierarchy of Needs* reveals a spectrum of motivations, which you may find helpful in your journey. I have taken from Maslow's work and from others to develop my own model for ambitions maturity continuum that I call the Ladder to Legacy. I use the acronym SWAT—Survival, Wellness, Abundance, and Transcendence.

As a younger man, I dreamt of being a world-class philanthropist. I saw a world of people in desperate need of love, compassion, and kindness, and I wanted to invest in making a profoundly positive impact in those lives. The only problem was that I was virtually penniless. I assumed that I would need to live the first part of my life as a "taker" to amass this fortune and then switch to become a "giver" when the time was right. My challenge was that I struggled to embrace the "taker" mindset. I found myself wanting to skip that stage and just become a master-giver. Finally I broke through to the awareness that all great fortunes and empires were built by individuals who had transcended self to invest themselves in ideas and purposes greater than themselves. I realized that I could be—and must become—a master-servant in order to amass that fortune. In fact, "deserve" means "from-service." Therefore, if you're not earning enough it's because you're not serving enough. I committed to delivering massive value at all times to open the floodgates of remuneration. I became so enthralled with this philanthropic vision that my dream shifted from giving a little bit of money from my envisioned "stack" of wealth, to only keeping what I need from the "stack" and watching it go to transform lives.

I'm not trying to suggest I'm a selfless saint, and I can learn to give more and consume less, but I want to share with you the vision that drives me.

This is what I would call Pure Ambition.

Compassionate contribution that flows from abundance without taxing wellness is the only sustainable Philanthropy.

Pure Adaptability

My early challenges, if they were to be managed and/or overcome, demanded that I face my reality, acknowledge my strengths, weakness, limitations, and opportunities. After facing my personal truth, I then required a functional paradigm of how this world works. At the time, I felt that the world was designed to fit someone else. The third step was to find a way to adapt my "truth" to the "truths" of how this world works. I reasoned that if I could adapt, find my own unique path to a life worth living, it may, in the end, seem as if my challenges, limitations, and trials were all part of an unfair advantage.

Here again is my three-part suggestion:

1. Find out and face your truth. I'm suggesting a full and accurate self-analysis including the good, the bad and the ugly.

2. Find or develop a functional philosophy and/or paradigm of how this world works.

3. Work to create an adaptive strategy that manages and makes the most of your uniqueness.

I sincerely believe all of our "uniqueness" is for a reason and in its right place, employed the right way, your limitations and challenges become your unfair advantages.

As I mentioned earlier, I have ADHD, and as a child I had to go to speech therapy classes because I was almost impossible to understand. I could not string together an intelligent sentence (some say I'm still struggling). I also struggled greatly with self-esteem, making friends, emotional self-regulation, and virtually all elements of Emotionally Intelligent (EQ) communications. Because these were uniquely painful challenges, I developed a unique fascination with the related sciences and philosophies. I learned deeply and eventually developed my ability to not only raise my experience from below the societal norms to meet these norms, but to eventually become one of the world's most sought out experts on these topics. ADHD makes me uniquely aware of the audience's interests and engagement levels, thereby turning my "curse" into my "blessing." In honor of this process, my company is named EQ Communications Inc.

The happiest people on this planet are the people who are living on purpose.

I suggest you continually work, rework, refine, and adapt your unique strategy to ensure you live your best possible life. Darwin's theory of evolution suggests the species most likely to survive is not the fastest, biggest, or the most powerful. The species most likely to survive is the most adaptable. If you are adaptable, you are unstoppable.

Pure Persistence

It's going to get messy, but remember, "It's not over until it's over!"

Plan to make this the greatest life possible. Plan to work through whatever you must work through. Plan to get back up when you fall. Plan to forgive yourself when you blow it. Plan to forgive others when they let you down. Plan to do whatever it takes. Plan to persist. Plan to adjust, revisit, rethink, retool, reframe, refocus, recommit, and re-launch.

Life is tough; life is unfair; and there's no free lunch.

Your best possible chance at your best possible life is to be the best possible you!

With pure ambition, pure adaptability, and pure persistence, you will enjoy your best possible life!

James MacNeil

James MacNeil is a world-renowned communications expert dedicated to helping people "Be More, Do More, Have More and Give More." He is founder and author of *Verbal Aikido*—Pure Communications Mastery, a life-transforming communications skillset and philosophy. He's a widely popular sales trainer and motivational speaker, and a highly valued consultant to some of the worlds' most successful banks and corporations. James is the author of the upcoming books, *The Guru Builder* and *Verbal Aikido*. James MacNeil has addressed more than sixteen hundred live audiences and has shared the stage with mega-brands such as Anthony Robbins, Rudy Giuliani, Les Brown, Steve Forbes, Robert Allen, Larry King, T. Harv Eker and Sir Richard Branson.

People First, Before Anything

By Jey Jeyakanthan

Growing up in Sri Lanka in the small village of Kokuvil, Jaffna, I never thought that I would one day get the opportunity to run a successful business, or even be offered the chance to gain the education that my career has been built on. In the area where I grew up, success was measured by your ability to survive the day, and safety bunkers were an essential element of every house structure. You learned very quickly not to develop ambitions or goals, because there was no guarantee of a future in which you could pursue them. Having knowledge in Kokuvil attributed to your ability to run for your life at any given moment. If your family was still together the following day, you had achieved the ultimate success. You never considered looking at your life as part of a bigger picture because living moment-to-moment was considered an achievement within itself.

Sadly, my best friend while growing up decided that he wanted to become part of the rebel group that was attacking my hometown village. He joined those forces and because of this ambition, lost his life at the tender age of thirteen. His passing was one of much devastation that I faced in Sri Lanka as a young man. I lost a lot of people who, although were not blood related, were individuals I considered family. With each death that occurred, I felt that I had not only experienced the disappearance of the person themselves, but also of a very important aspect of my life. I still become overwhelmed with emotions on occasion when I think of these moments. It is amazing how, although so far in the past, these times still feel like yesterday.

When I was a late teen my family was blessed with the ability to move to Canada. Coming to this country was a whole new world for me and I had to learn to surrender to the fact that I was not under constant attack. While most teens my age immersed themselves in a life filled with organized sports, clubs, and yearbooks, I struggled with coming to terms with the fact that my new friends would not end up turning around and attacking my home when I least expected it. Not being afforded the same pleasures that Canadian children had growing up, I also had to learn that it was more than acceptable to borrow books from the library and bring them home, that it was normal to own more than a few outfits, and that a free education was something I now was fortunate to have. Once I realized what I had been given, I decided to take the opportunity and use it to its full advantage.

After I completed high school, I moved onwards to college and then attended university. It was during this time that I not only met my beautiful wife, Vahini, who I have now been married to for sixteen years, but I started to see my life take a whole different turn. I also discovered that I had unharnessed potential, where if I worked hard enough, I would have the ability to achieve goals and dreams that I would never before thought would be possible. As I began to start a family of my own, I was also determined to give my daughters, Aarthi and Arani, the life that I never had growing up. I wanted to immerse my daughters with the strong family values that provided me with hope during the most difficult times. I never imagined, however, that these bonds would be tested again so soon.

When one of my daughters was born, she had to overcome a sensitive surgery that was essential for her survival. As a father, it was a hard time for me and my family and it was difficult to remain positive despite this devastating situation. Being granted her wellbeing and health is one of the greatest miracles I have ever witnessed and has again reminded me of the importance of family ties. In fact, my wife and I now fundraise for Sick Kids Hospital with the hope that this miracle will touch other families with sick children, as well.

Although I said before that growing up in such a traumatic area did not breed children like myself with strong passions and goals, what I didn't realize was that at the time I was learning the most important business lesson of all—the value of people. Watching those who I loved vanish before me in Sri Lanka taught me from a young age that time on this earth is not something that is guaranteed. I also learned that every person who comes in and out of your life, whether they enrich or challenge you, play an essential role in your life story. Looking back now, I can see how this lesson helped me to found my current company, AVAJ Future Solutions. I know that I still carry this knowledge with me and that it plays a major role in my daily decisions.

My heart continues to be and always will be toward the people who uproot their lives and come to Canada. I understand that everyone has value, no matter what their background. Every person has overcome a transition of change in order to achieve their goals and dreams. At AVAJ Future Solutions we pick staff members who need to gain credibility, training, and expertise. We take them in as apprentices and provide them with the hours and knowledge needed to pursue high quality and well-paying jobs following their education. We also endorse them as valuable members of the IT profession following their training. We try to help our staff attend motivational speaking and self-development training so that they can continue to grow in their personal lives and in their careers. Since I was not afforded the motivational materials, television, or books to empower and encourage my dreams, I plan to make this information accessible to every person I can. I guess you can say that I see the diamond in every individual and just want to provide them with the support they need to shine.

Giving back is also an essential aspect of realizing the value of people. Again, I think that everyone has the ability to pursue great things; however, some are not afforded the opportunity to do so. My business is involved with organizations such as Amnesty International, The Sophia Hilton Foundation of Canada, and The Heart and Stroke Foundation. This, however, is only the tip of the iceberg. As AVAJ Future Solutions grows, I hope that my ability to give back can also grow. AVAJ sponsors my daughter's holding school, as well, by donating tablets and supporting the school council in their endeavour to bring school instruments in to assist children. I am also personally involved in the political arena and understand its importance in driving change. I want my daughters to learn the value of giving back to the community and hope that they live with the understanding that opportunities occur when you choose to always leave doors open.

I am also drawn to positive and authentic people who are ambitious and who pursue things for the greater good. I truly believe that the universe is a sincere thing and will give you what you put out there. I always try to see the good in others and I think that being a business-minded individual has provided me with an ability to see the wide range of opportunities that every connection provides. Again, I believe that there is so much value in every individual and because of that I never shut myself off to any person who wants to interact with me. We have so much to learn from each other when we are open to just being a nice person. I wake up every day excited about who I may possibly meet or what I will learn next.

Even though we are considered the top Internet Technology Company in Toronto and have many elite clientele, my passion is still to help and assist small business owners so they can take their operation to the next level. Our method of business has allowed us to acquire highly skilled staff members that are as passionate about making a difference as I am. No matter how big our company grows, this is something that we will strive to keep in our DNA. It defines who we are, not only as a business, but as individuals. I believe that authenticity is the key to good business and I know that people want to work with us as it is clear that we love what we do. AVAJ hopes to inspire others to run their business with the same passion and drive that we strive for every day.

Although certain circumstances in my life have not been easy, to be honest, I wouldn't have had it any other way. I believe that people are truly a measure of their ability to take anything life throws at them and turn it into opportunity. There are going to be bumps in the road as I continue throughout life, but I know to not view them negatively, but rather to see them as a chance to learn something new and meet new people. With this in mind, this is what I believe to be the three most important pieces of wisdom to live by:

1. Find your passion and work hard. This will always bring you happiness and success.

2. Don't be afraid of failure—and never quit.

3. Constantly network and never stop improving. Use tools like social media to assist you in this mission.

I truly believe that everyone on this earth, no matter who they are, was put here to change the world and leave a legacy for the next generation. My family truly accomplished this. I will not rest until I do the same in my life, for my family, and for my business. What I am most looking forward to, however, is who I will meet and what I have left to experience on this journey. One thing I know for sure is that if you put people first, you have already achieved the greatest success.

Jey Jeyakanthan

Jey is a highly successful entrepreneur and IT professional with over twenty-two years of experience in Business Development, Project Management, and Business Transformation for Fortune-200 companies. Jey is actively involved with many volunteer and advocacy organizations in Canada and currently holds the position of Director for the Sophia Hilton Foundation of Canada. He was also a member of Markham Board of Trade and Canadian Tamils' Chamber of Commerce.

In 2011, Jey founded *AVAJ Future Solutions*. AVAJ is a Toronto-based company specializing in the creation of Mobile Apps Development and Web Design. As AVAJ's leading authority on mobile strategy, he defines the stages of mobile marketing evolution and works with clients to achieve the best objectives for mobile marketing. He helps business owners and entrepreneurs develop their mobile marketing practices, and successfully engages their increasingly mobile customers in an authentic and professional manner. Jey also brings with him his expertise and extensive experience in Social Media and Search Engine Optimization, which gives him a powerful understanding of how these complementary technologies can be used together to effectively bring marketers and customers ever closer together.

Jey is also an active contributor to the local political arena and holds position as Member of Campaign Advisory Committee, Strategic Planner, and Reporter.

Jey and his wife, Vahini, have two children, Aarthi and Arani Jeyakanthan, and have been happily married for sixteen years.

He can be reached at jey@avaj.ca and you can visit his website at www.avaj.ca

The Illusion of Self-Worth

By Jordan Ovejas aka Mr. Magic

That moment, when we witness something for the first time and it completely astonishes us to the point where we're left speechless, and the only words that manage to escape our wide open jaw is, "How did you do that?" That was my exact reaction the first time I witnessed magic. However, unlike most people who just want to know how it's done so they don't feel confused, I really wanted to know so that I could create that same experience for people anytime, anywhere. I started on that journey and never looked back. For most of the audience reading this book, I'm sure they say they are not willing to dedicate the hours and hours and hours' worth of practicing in front of a mirror, recording, and messing up in front of live audiences. So I'm going to save you all the trouble, and instead of going into depth on how I do all my tricks, I'll teach one secret that most magicians use but don't say they do with all their magic. It might seem really simple, but it's truly what got me to where I am right now. If you're ready for it, let's go for a ride down memory lane along this magical journey of Mr. Magic and uncover the secret along the way!

Let's go back to 1998 when I was standing in the third-grade class of my new school and feeling so alone. I did not know a soul in the room, and I remember just before class started there was one kid walking around the class pointing at people saying, "I know you, I know you, I know you..." and turns to me and says, "I don't know you." And then turns away. Right after he did that I thought to myself, "Am I not important? Am I not worthy to be liked? Just because he doesn't know me? I have to be known and liked." In that moment I made a decision to myself subconsciously that I would never feel left out again. Therefore, the solution I had in my mind was just to get along with everyone and be the joker in the class. That was the value I was offering to the class—one of a joker—someone who makes people laugh and feel good. This worked for a while, until I was doing things in my life because I felt I had to please everyone, and truly that was never going to work because I wasn't doing what I wanted.

Fast forward to 2003 when I see my buddy show me the very first form of close-up magic I've ever seen. And after he did it I thought, "There's definitely something here for me to learn. I gotta figure it out!" He said, "Here's three rows of seven cards; mentally pick a card and point to the row your card is in." He takes the other row, then takes the row I pointed to, then finishes the pile with the last row, repeats this two more times and then he says, "Okay I'm going to count out ten cards and to the eleventh card name your card out loud." So he goes, "One! Two! Three!..." finally to the eleventh card and says, "Name your card out loud!" I tell him seven of clubs and he turns over the card and low and behold, it's my card! I literally grabbed the card out of his hand and started examining the deck.

That night I started researching and I learned that trick. I showed it to someone in my family, got a good response, then I learned another one, and another one, until it became an obsession. Once I got really confident about a certain illusion I learned, I would then take it to people in high school, and practice live performances on them. In my mind at the time, I thought, "The only way to really fit in to this high school crowd is to impress people so much with my magic that no one can judge me or say anything bad about me. I'll be known as the magician." Every time I met someone new, magic was somehow brought into the equation, even until today. However, now I do it for a different purpose, which I'll get to in a second. Again, even though I felt like I was "The Magician" in my school, for some reason I still didn't feel like a million bucks. I still felt some sort of unworthiness. Something was missing.

Three years later, I met some really friendly people that came to my parent's house during the spring and they eventually invited me out to a youth retreat hosted by a Catholic organization called *BNP, Banal Na Pagaaral* (translated means Holy Studies). This was the first time I attended something where I went away to the States for a weekend and my parents were a little sceptical, thinking I may be kidnapped or something. I understood because of how many hundreds of hours of news they watch bombarding them with negative stories. I still ended up going, and aside from all the unknowingness of what was going to happen, it ended up being a life transformational weekend. At the end, when all of us had to share how we felt after, I felt really good being up in front of a microphone and speaking to a crowd. I was up there for a few minutes at least, had no clue what I said after and then I remember people coming up to me afterwards saying, "Wow, Jordan, that was a powerful sharing. Thanks for volunteering to share your experience because it truly made an impact on my life." When I heard those words for the first time, I just said, "Oh, thank you!" Like I was in surprise, and as I kept doing more and more speeches in front of audiences, I realized that this is the value that I want to hold in society—one who creates an impact on people's lives to really act in spirit, as opposed to in lack. Soon I started to feel as if I had a bigger mission to fill. I didn't know what it was yet, however. I just had a feeling.

The following year I got involved with my very first Multi-Level Marketing business at the age of seventeen and this was the start of my Personal Development Journey. Fast forward to the time between 2007-2014; I'd participated in all different types of sales from business to business, face-to-face marketing, telemarketing, while doing network marketing on the side. I'd gained all this knowledge on one thing, which was, "Who am I and what am I called to do?" Finally one day in the summer of 2014, a friend of mine really kicked me in the butt and said, "Look, you've been practicing and performing magic for almost twelve years now and you're really good at what you do. Stop wasting your talent and start getting paid for your efforts!" It really hit me at that time because I'd been working on a job that was starting to get redundant, and I was only doing it for the money. Now I was at a point where I knew I had something great here.

With all the knowledge I had attained from sales and marketing, the personal development as well as the magic, my value in this marketplace should be in the millions, if not more! What I really came to realize is that the value I put on myself will determine how I position myself in the marketplace, and how others will then see me. Cut it out with the unworthiness crap! I deserve to be paid in the millions for the value I provide to my clients or fans. After this pivotal moment, I decided to drop any other side business I had going on, and just completely focus on the magic.

Realizing the talents and skills I had combined with sales and marketing and magic, I've come to the belief that I'm called to touch, move, and inspire millions of youth around the world to pursue their passions using magic and public speaking combined for something called inspirational magic. So I'm sure by now most of the readers are wondering, "Okay, nice story, but what's the secret?" If some of you were paying attention to the story, you'll notice that anytime I adopted a new belief I became that which I thought about myself. The first step to doing magic is to actually believe that you can perform and do magic. Not only for yourself, but for others as well, anywhere, anytime. Therefore, what I realized is, first determine and truly get a true picture of the person I want to become. Once I had that image, I started adding deep emotional connection with it as if it had already been present in my life. I started acting on it and I realized that people, situations, and circumstances started coming into my life to validate the belief that I so strongly held in my mind of who I was.

The magic is in believing first before seeing. The biggest illusion that I had for the longest time was that I had to see it in order to believe it. Magicians and visionaries believe before they see. Determine which side you want to be on: belief or fear? Have a magical day!

www.facebook.com/jordanovejas, instagram: @whatsyourmagic, youtube: whatsyourmagic

Jordan Ovejas aka Mr. Magic

Jordan Ovejas, aka Mr. Magic, born and raised in Mississauga, Ontario, Canada. Now Twenty-four-years-old, he has had quite the magical journey up to this point. Jordan has been practicing and performing the art of magic and illusions since 2003. He has also been a leading sales trainer for direct sales in the last three years. Combining both skills and experiences from sales and magic, he has coined himself to be an inspirational magician performing shows, hosting events, and workshops that astonish, inspire, and empower young people ages 13-35 to pursue their passion and live the life they truly desire. Magic to Jordan is a way to connect with the audience on an intimate level; he uses it as a tool to empower those who attend his events to see life from a different perspective and break any limiting beliefs. "Limits, like fear, are often just an illusion."

Finding You... a Dance of Courage Back Home to your Authentic Beauty

By Josephine Auciello

"Papa, I wanna be a dancer." The look on my dad's face said it all. I knew he was thinking, "Where did I go wrong?" I could tell that he was searching my eyes to assess whether or not I was *really* serious. But I was and he felt it. My father immigrated to Canada to give his family the chance at a better life than what he had endured. He knew this meant hard work and he wasn't shy to that in the slightest. Without even speaking full English he worked two jobs right from the start and soon afterward started his own business during the day while holding another job at night. Slowly but surely, he rose up to create a life of stability that he knew would support his loved ones through any storm. His desire was to pass this knowledge to us, his children. He knew this meant he needed to teach us how to build a solid foundation and learn the value of structure. Following your passion was not part of that equation from his perspective. I, however, was a little girl deeply aligned to my essence. I knew what gave me pleasure and made my heart sing. When I danced, when I was creative, I came alive and I felt glorious—even beautiful.

I was not unique in my "knowing." Most of us also "know"…when we are little…

What I often find today as an adult woman working with adult women in my coaching practice, is that most of us as little girls started out aligned to our truth, yet we'd somehow lost pieces of ourselves along the way to the "now." Now being in a place that symbolizes having "arrived" to somewhere amazing, somewhere happy—majestic even—that's the proposed promise of working toward our futures of happiness, the wonderment lies in arriving to a certain destination. Nothing could be further from the truth. It took many trials and tribulations along my own journey in life to fully understand this, then more time and effort to actually embody it. The little girl who knew exactly what path to take succumbed to the pressures from "out there" when she was little and gave her power away because she didn't know any other way. She wasn't even aware that she had a choice. A part of her got buried inside as she dutifully followed her parent's wishes, her culture's norms, and her society's role models for "success." To be successful meant you followed the "rules" of society. To be beautiful meant you followed what the advertisers showed you. Success was a "thing"; beauty was something to be "obtained."

What I've learned today and what I teach my clients is that success is not a cookie-cutter recipe. Beauty is not what the magazines want to make us believe. We "know" this yet we don't fully believe it. We still fall prey to the myth. True success is being aligned to the truth of who we authentically are and from this alignment our true beauty radiates.

Do you ever see a woman walk into a room and all of a sudden it seems as if the lights got brighter? It is her truth that is speaking to us. It is her truth that radiates, not the clothes she wears or the makeup she chose to put on that morning. She has taken a stand for her truth; she is aligned to her truth and she embodies it. That's what draws us in. That's how we each are meant to express ourselves in the world—to express our divine beauty. It starts from being connected to our truest self. That comes from searching deep within. That comes from acknowledging what gave us pleasure as children. That comes from having courage to re-discover, to reconnect, and then restore this essence.

The myth about beauty is that it comes from outside you, and other people can apply its standards to you and judge you by them. This isn't real beauty. It's a lie and lies are always ugly. Beauty comes from alignment to our truest self.

Just as our physical bodies rely on alignment for balance, strength, and grace, our inner selves have a proper alignment as well. Every person has their own inner truth, the essence of who they are and who they are meant to become. There is something in us that we are meant to do, which resonates with the song of our own beauty and which we are meant to live in line with. It is the framework of our inner being, just as if our bones form a framework for our physical bodies, and just as our bones give us physical structure, this inner truth gives us *real* structure to our lives.

At least it should. Sadly, many women are unaware of their internal truth and they try to find it by living according to external standards. They give their power away. They ask for external validation and believe what they hear from others as a stronger truth than what their own heart is trying to tell them. They apply external structure to their lives. Over time, they lose track of their own inner truth. So many of us ignore or even abuse our own inner essence. Real beauty is not found by breaking one's inner truth to reshape it into someone else's ideal. Real success and real beauty come from when we find our own inner truth and align ourselves with it.

I talk to so many women today, and I realize that many of us are successful in so many areas of our lives—well at least according to standards set by society. We have good careers, we make good income, we have our homes, our children, our families, or whatever the case may be, yet what I hear most is that something is still missing. They are not hitting that bull's eye. They feel incomplete somehow. Their sense of purpose is not whole. This is their cue to start the real search, to go back in time to return with the real pearls of wisdom. This is a journey of courage and the fruits will most definitely be the most rewarding.

When a woman finds and embodies her own inner truth and learns to align herself with it, she becomes radiant. She becomes beautiful from the inside out. Life becomes infused with joy and love. She wastes less energy and has more energy to pursue what she truly loves to do. Stress drains from her body, and the smiles are natural and full. She is able to love herself more deeply and others in her life, as well.

She becomes magnetic. She draws others to her. She becomes a reflection to other women of what is possible for them, as well. She reflects back to them their own truth.

How do we align ourselves with our inner truth? First we have to find it. Some women are fortunate in having a sense of it, some women are not sure, and others feel they have no idea. In each case, the process is the same. In order to find your inner truth you must engage your intuition. How many of us ignore our intuitive messages and allow logic to rule? Intuition is our greatest guiding force. Engaging our intuition empowers us. It takes courage to search our hearts to find our essence. The modern world doesn't teach us how to make friends with our deepest knowing. We, in fact, are often taught to ignore these messages. It keeps us too busy and surrounds us with noise and confusion. We get so often easily distracted. It takes real courage to look inside when one is not sure what is in there. We are afraid of what we might find, of what we might uncover. What if we uncover some wounds that still need healing? That's the thing, until we *do* search inside we will never free ourselves from these wounds that do require healing—that's the courage part. Healing is never as traumatic as the experience first was. Engaging our courage to look within and heal the wounds that *may* or may not exist in there gives us the opportunity to see the opposite and get in touch with our real essence, to free her so we stop feeling as if something is *still* missing. Real beauty is inside us; the myth is the ugly imposter.

How do we look inside if we've never done so? How do we start? It all sounds pretty mystical and fanciful. One of the easiest and fastest ways is to engage our creativity. Our creativity gives us a practical place to start because we can access our intuition through a tangible start. The creative process helps us get out of our logical mind and discover ourselves. When we are being creative, we connect to our deepest self. You know you are fully engaged when you lose track of time and become so enraptured that you can hear the magical intuitive voice the loudest without interference.

Creativity is one of the ways we can get in touch with our souls. We learn to trust and love ourselves. We learn who we are, individually and uniquely, and see the beauty that no one else holds because it belongs to us.

When we engage our intuition and creativity, and when we follow them with courage into our inner truth, we learn how to become aligned to our truest essence. Over time, we then learn how to live out of our essence instead of the other way around. We discover our truest path and purpose. That's when we find true joy and peace and that's when we radiate our unique beauty, both of spirit and of body. It is transformative. It reaches out and changes the world around us. By first discovering love and trust for ourselves, we can then open the way for love and trust between others, too. This is the path of real beauty and purpose: to grow, to learn, to be creative, to support each other, and to become radiant in our own unique truth and love. Where in your own life can you reconnect to parts of your truth that holds your authentic beauty? It is a dance of courage, not for the faint hearted yet one that yields the highest form of joy ... and isn't that the way life was meant to be lived?

Josephine Auciello

Josephine Auciello is a women's empowerment and relationship coach, entrepreneur, author, mom of two, and lover of life. She supports women entrepreneurs to transform relationship blocks into breakthroughs that can help them reach their dreams while deeply embodying their feminine wisdom to create more beauteous, rich, and fulfilling lives. Josephine helps women redefine what's possible for them in life, love, and business. She turns the often serious struggles women face with their partners during times of deep personal transformation into gifts that enlighten and empower both parties so they can experience greater love, harmony, grace, and fulfillment through a woman's empowerment process. She works with women one-on-one, as well as with couples, and runs men's groups that empower the principles of conscious communication in relationships. She teaches worldwide the art of love and dynamics of masculine and feminine power.

Josephine co-authored a book with three New York Times Bestselling Authors and has been mentored by many greats like Marci Shimoff, Chris Attwood and Janet Attwood, Gina DeVee, Joe Garcia, and Annie Lalla. She's now on a mission to guide other women to overcome their blocks in love and business so they can live life to their fullest on their own terms. She leads feminine wisdom retreats in Greece and Italy, and is devoted to helping every woman uncover her natural beauty, wisdom, and purpose in a spirit of love.

Miracles Do Happen

By Kamil C. Kowalski

"Let's go celebrate!" I exclaimed enthusiastically on Friday at 6 p.m. in our cozy downtown Toronto office, just minutes after officially closing a lengthy Software Project on a chilly February afternoon.

"Ok, what're you thinking?" asked my friend and business partner.

"Let's go Blue Mountain. Been a while since we skied last. And it's nearly the end of the season," I replied.

"Sounds good! But let's go early this time. Do more of Day skiing. We always go late. When? Sunday?"

"Sure! Let's leave after nine. We should be able to start by noon."

Little did I know that that Sunday of 2008 would be the day that the Universe would officially decide to change the direction of my life—as per my own request, mind you, just four short months earlier.

Everything had started out so well.

At twenty-one, I had found my soul mate and experienced true love. I graduated from the University of Toronto with a skill of communicating in twenty-three computer languages. While holding the hot-off-the-press diploma still in my hand, I had decided to instate my first IT Solutions Company.

Within the second year of being with the firm, our team of three had been delivering cutting edge enterprise solutions to large corporate clients. The year-end revenue of 1.2 million dollars in sales was driven primarily by pure joy and adrenaline! Perhaps I was onto something here…

Eventually, however, the stress of 80-120-hour workweeks and ever-growing clients' expectations had started to have its toll on me. Not just the overall exhaustion due to the lack of the work-life balance, but also my weight gain and the increasing number of health challenges.

I felt as if I was caught in a hamster wheel, cranking out solutions one after another, but seeing no end in sight. My true love connection didn't survive this madness either.

Something needed to change…

It was in November of 2007 that I happened to watch the movie "The Secret." Just as it was for millions of people, it too had a huge impact on me. I felt a nudge that this whole "Law of Attraction" and "Feeling Good" were somehow the key to a happier life.

I made the intention to change my life—mainly to live more joyfully every day! In my notebook I composed a Vision Board of cheerful friends, tranquil places, fit models, wise people, and various depictions of financial abundance.

Almost immediately a new kind of people entered my life, referencing things like yoga, meditation, energy, vibration, Chakras, and the like. But because I liked the vibe of this secret world and felt a calling to invest more time studying it, I soon made many positive friends and met a few spiritual masters.

Yet, I continued my double fulltime commitment to the corporation because it made more sense for the "day-to-day living demands" at that time. Talk about a conflict of interests!

And so on that Sunday of February 2008, right after the completion of the large project, my life path was abruptly adjusted in the form of a serious skiing accident.

I crashed at the end of my last run breaking a small bone adjacent to my C1 vertebrae. The situation wasn't pretty, so by midnight I was air-lifted to a Toronto hospital. I was a veggie for a few days; however, I strongly believed that this couldn't be the end. I had made that intention recently, hadn't I?

Lying in the hospital bed, I vividly remembered Morris E. Goodman, the man in "The Secret" who crashed his plane. Just like his, my recovery was supported by the emergency healthcare and by the power of my mind: I believed… NO! I "knew" my way to wellness. My new spiritual friends had also been helping by sending me healing energy in-person and remotely.

On day three, I made my first efforts to walk around despite the strong protest of the nurses, making the unofficial hospital news with the headline "Who *is* this guy?!"

On day seven, my neck brace was removed because the CAT scan showed no sign of damage.

On day ten, I was transferred to a physiotherapy center for a couple of weeks to regain mobility in my seized neck. I also had sessions of a special form of ancient Chinese acupuncture, which was especially helpful in releasing the clutched muscles.

The intensity of the healing experience, in addition to a warm and peaceful energy surrounding me, compelled me to phase out my worldly business. I've embarked on a years-long journey to understand the significance and the truth behind this orchestrated gift of a second chance in life.

In fact, what I didn't completely realize at that time was that I was guided to become a vibrational match to what I was asking for with my intention. In other words, to consciously evolve into the person that is, acts, and feels with every cell of my being like the best version of who I was meant to be.

Fast forward six years to a time beyond immense amounts of often magical inner healing work, total body-mind overhaul, DNA adjustments, and getting to know myself better including the Godly part of who we truly are.

Today, in mid-November, I'm chillin' at a small Café in sunny and warm San Diego, California. I'm sipping on a delicious frothy cappuccino and savoring amazing coconut macaroons. Across from me sits my new awesome and beautiful girl—another soul mate—because yes, there can be more than one.

I'm enjoying refreshing sights and sounds of the Pacific Ocean shore, being completely in the present moment of now, feeling truly happy, and serenely at peace with the world, knowing all is well.

The moment is infused with appreciation and gratitude for how far I've come in the recent years: health repair, weight loss, business and sales training, transformation of family relationships, and exuberant encounters with beautiful and fascinating women in touch with their personal power and feminine side—to mention a few highlights. But the most impactful changes in my life are the financial and the invisible.

In the shadows of the 2008 global economic crisis, I went from bleeding and losing tens of thousands of dollars, declaring partial personal bankruptcy, and being technically unemployable, to living below the poverty line on welfare and in community housing, for which, too, I am very grateful.

I turned things around in five months, when I was ready, and I made a firm decision to do so. With a couple of quick certifications and an application of the Pareto's 80/20 Rule, I focused on top business activities and top paying clients. The results were a more peaceful mind and my best client eagerly securing and renewing a six-figure contract with a 12.5 per cent premium per annum.

What are my Secret Key Lessons from this wild ride?

1. Stop the bleeding, get some cash in the door, and come up for air to think.

2. Strategy over Persistence. After sending over three hundred resumes with no luck due to outdated education and no "real job" experience, I had a wake-up call. I stepped back and thought about the fastest and most effective way to the biggest cash in order to quickly repay my outstanding debts and resurrect my life.

3. In-Demand Value-Add. I researched the current IT job market by studying salaries of various top positions, the most frequent requirements within job postings, and required certifications that would take the least time and effort to acquire.

4. Show and Tell. While casting a wide net for full time jobs, contracts, and clients, I've prepared all my previous work results in a professional portfolio. In the meetings I would use a combination of my recently upgraded people, presentation, and negotiation skills for maximum impact.

5. Image and Awareness. Focus and determination were my strong skills, but they needed to be balanced with self-awareness. The impact of my image and behavior needed to be focused on creating trust and likeability, thus improving the effectiveness of team collaboration and my to-be leadership.

6. Magic of Positive Attitude. Not only did I consistently deliver high quality output from the place of service, but I enhanced it further by making people's jobs easier with helpful add-ons. The words of appreciation such as "Thank You," small uplifting comments with a smile, and non-verbal greetings and nods further create unbelievable and lasting results.

7. Self-Respect and Integrity. Occasionally, I go beyond the call of duty, stay longer, or deliver over-the-top. However, as I've learned the hard way in my first company, it is critical to manage expectations, protect boundaries, and ensure that I communicate these extras in a diplomatic and clear manner. The kicker is that people value and respect confident integrity more than freebies.

8. It *is* about the Relationships. I naturally make solid relationships with key people in power or stay closely connected to people in power. I take a bit of time to be interested in their personal lives and offer interesting or relevant news about my life from time to time, always being professional and respectful, yet also cool and easy-going. I take time to understand their job and what is important to them, and I strive to always make them look good in front of others. I ask good questions or make on-point statements, and sometimes I challenge them about their conclusions or position, but always respectfully and/or in private.

9. **Many Ways to Riches.** Money is simply a tool for exchanging *value*. Whether it's service, product, or information, you exchange what resonates with you as valuable. Money is not power. Money, like everything, is energy. Therefore, it is important to come to money from a place of positive emotions such as playfulness or caring.

That ninth point brings me to the next key change in my life: living in harmony with the rhythm of life where the Universe is at work helping me realize my dreams. This is the invisible magic of synchro-destiny—a term coined by Deepak Chopra in his book "The Seven Spiritual Laws of Success."

Synchro-destiny brings together seemingly unrelated events that bring fulfillment to our lives. It's an alignment with the flow of the Universe where coincidences and mini-miracles show up almost daily, and opportunities and helpful encounters arise out of the blue.

I enjoy this magic of the Universe tremendously. It is amusing to witness the playfulness of the Universe, how it tweaks the reality to spawn certain arrangements of situations and information, while making it believable to the uninitiated. Then after delivering the results, it's almost as if the Universe nudges my arm with an excited grin, and says, "So? How did you like this one? Pretty cool, yes?"

Just as I was getting here to the café, I received not one or two, but three interesting and "out of the blue" emails. First is a request to advertise a certain health service on my blog, which I will need to review for alignment later. Second is a casting call for a commercial shoot in the Caribbean with a daily rate, airfare and stay paid by the production company. (awesome!) Finally the third is a high quality, personally written email with an offer to write articles for my websites.

Just like a pilot who is about to take off and knows where he's going, you need to be very clear and focused too, in order to get to where you're going. Everything that you desire will come to you effortlessly as long as you set a clear intention—a clear understanding of what you *do* want to have happen—feel enthusiastic about it, believe in the possibility, it serves you and others, and brings harm to no one.

So what do you really want, either right now just for fun, or long-term as the dream career? What do you want to learn? Is there any particular experience you want to have, or some "unfinished business" that, like a boomerang, keeps returning into your field of longings or fantasies?

Maybe you crave more than what the material world can offer you? Something that deep within you needs to be fulfilled? Maybe you're interested in finding out who you really are? For underneath many layers of life habituations and emotional build-ups there you are, happier and lighter, basking in the bliss of God or *your true Higher Self*, where you are wholly taken care of and live as you want to.

Ask yourself those questions and listen in silence to your heart for answers. You can also ask for clarity and guidance in prayer to Angels, Archangels, or Saints, and then receive the valuable "intel" as visions, sounds, feelings, or other "signs" in your dreams, meditations, or in your daily life.

Anything's possible! Once you know what you want, feel it deeply and trust that the Universe has heard you and is moving you toward it. Take the first step that makes the most sense, be it Googling or going about your day with eyes and ears open in search of the right people who can help you get there.

I am thrilled to share that the Universe has supported the fulfillment of my outstanding bucket list items in the recent twenty-four months. Many were accessed at a very low cost or on a basis of a win-win value exchange.

The most exciting experiences include learning to drive sideways in a BMW M3 (drifting), racing a Lamborghini, Ferrari, and Porsche, and flying a Boeing 777 and Fighter Jet (in a professional simulator). Also acting in two TV Series as a soldier and as a general, doing stunts, learning Krav Maga martial arts, and a few others including enjoying blissful tantric experiences.

> *"It is confidence in our bodies, minds, and spirits that allows us to keep looking for new adventures, new directions to grow in, and new lessons to learn—which is what life is all about."*
> – Oprah Winfrey
> (About Entertainment: Oprah Winfrey)

Happiness is an inside job first! Be a good friend to yourself and always steer towards a better feeling place. Follow your joy and allow miracles to happen because as you do, you will inspire others—from family and friends, to community, city, and nation—and eventually the World.

For it is through the balance of the heart and intuition with the mind and science, plus an application of the Universal Laws of the cosmos, that we can purposely and consciously co-create with spirit our own individual realities, and in turn, architect a new level of consciousness for humanity.

Quotes:

"You have time to do everything that needs to be done and it will be done when the time is right. Possibly sooner."
– Kamil C. Kowalski

"Happiness is the key to success. You have to love what you are doing."
– Albert Schweitzer

"Before You Assume – Learn; Before You Judge – Understand; Before You Hurt – Feel; Before You Say – Think."
– Kamil C. Kowalski's Reiki Master

"Kamil C. Kowalski illustrates different types of strengths that reside within each of us, and how we can access them when we need to change what no longer fits in our lives. He awakens the desire to identify with our own spirituality, and explore, recognize and initiate within ourselves that, which will bring us happiness."
– Kamil C. Kowalski's Reiki Master

Lifestyle Management Experts
Entrepreneur & Happiness Life Coach
www.PracticalWellness.ca

Kamil C. Kowalski

Kamil C. Kowalski brings out the best in smart people and guides them toward lasting happiness. He has a unique way of coaching and reaching results with clients—leveraging non-judgmental "I get you" understanding, effective brainstorming, practical coaching, and connection with the Higher Angelic wisdom.

Kamil has been an author, speaker, certified life coach, Reiki practitioner, and a seasoned entrepreneur since 2003. With his businesses, blog, and everyday presence, he inspires and empowers thousands of people to take immediate and direct action steps to enjoy better, happier, and more fulfilling lives. He helps his clients to accomplish their dreams and goals in a healthy and holistic "downstream" manner.

Kowalski has invested more than twenty thousand hours in personal change work and spiritual practice, as well as in business and marketing. In 2012, Kamil was interviewed on the Oprah Winfrey Network, and in 2014 he was featured in the business section of the Toronto Star newspaper. He is known for his down-to-earth, grounded and centered, peaceful, and cheerful approach to life.

Please feel free to connect with Kamil C. Kowalski through any of his websites.

www.PracticalWellness.ca

Laura Bilotta's Three Nuggets of Wisdom

By Laura Bilotta

For most of us, business success doesn't occur overnight. It takes time to go from hopeful entrepreneur to established, and along the way many lessons are learned. My journey as founder of an event and matchmaking based dating company, Single in the City (SITC), began in 2002. I remember how exciting it was when SITC was merely a concept. I remember launching, thinking the sky's the limit. When the company began having success, I felt incredibly rewarded for all the hard work I had put into realizing my dream—to create a space where people could connect with each other and form lasting romantic relationships.

Anyone who has owned their own business for as long as I have—thirteen years—will tell you that they've learned quite a bit over the years. I'm no different. Every little success provides motivation and reassurance. Conversely, each little failure is a notice to adapt, evolve, and improve. I'd like to share three specific nuggets of wisdom I've learned along the way. I believe these three pieces of wisdom will help new entrepreneurs achieve their goals.

1. Don't Let People Intimidate You

It's very easy to be intimidated when you're new to business. For starters, most of the people you deal with will not be as new to business ownership as you are; therefore, they'll already be more hardened by their own experiences. And of course, there are always those who will attempt to take advantage of the new kid on the block. Don't let people intimidate you; the person you are intimidated by is only human.

Your biggest idol or the head of a company is only a human, after all. He or she may have family issues, daddy issues, mommy issues, insecurities, rocky personal relationships, or any number of issues. They have things they are trying to prove, obstacles they're trying to overcome, fears, a desire to impress others, bills to pay, or feelings they're trying to protect. They all pass gas and poop, have to shower to be clean, cry when they're sad, and do whatever else it is that makes all of us human. So, while it is essential to have respect for others, I'd strongly advise that you do not confuse giving respect with being intimidated. Hold your head up high and believe that you belong in business; that you're going to be successful and no one is going to get in your way.

Approach everyone with love.

My trick to losing the intimidation that I may potentially have from others is to assume that everyone likes me before I even meet them. And, I assume that they are lovable, too. It works. I find it amazing how quickly this technique can soften up even the harshest and scariest people. I shower people with kindness. In doing so, they don't have much of a chance to be mean to me in any way.

In a way, it's common sense. If you take the opposite approach and assume that people won't like you or want to work with you, you'll wear those fears, that intimidation, all over your face. And you'll scare people away, or perhaps even invite them to take advantage of you because they sense you are intimidated by them.

Believe in the good within yourself. Be the best you can be and others will see your greatness because you'll display it in a way they cannot miss.

Over time, and as you gain more experience, you'll see that there's no reason to be intimidated by others; you have way too much to give and you are open to all you wish to receive. So don't be afraid to approach people on a business level. Let others know all about your great ideas. If you don't ask you won't receive, and if you don't share your intelligent thoughts with the world, they'll remain stagnant inside your own head. In other words: *reach for the stars*. You'll be surprised at what people will give if you have the courage to ask.

I've never been afraid to approach people and ask them for things that will further improve my business. I've orchestrated cross promotions and various advertising tactics by simply asking my fellow entrepreneurs if they'd like to work together with me. Single in the City was practically built on cross promotion opportunities, and you'd be surprised at how many people are willing to scratch your back if you scratch theirs.

Don't be intimidated because the success of your new business venture is largely dependent on your ability to fearlessly ask questions and make connections that will fast track your endeavour.

2. Don't EVER Give Up, Unless You Have To

It's no secret that most new businesses fail within the first five years. That being said, it doesn't mean you'll fail, too. You can be a success story. And when times get tough in the early stages, don't give up unless you absolutely have to do so. And by "have to," I mean that you can't pay your bills or support your family.

A lot of new business owners go a year or two without even paying themselves. It happens. All profits are thrown back into the business in an attempt to survive. It's not easy in the beginning, for most of us. But hard work and dedication goes a long way toward achieving the ultimate goal of running a profitable, established company.

If you find yourself considering whether or not to quit, first consider other options. Get another job if you have to. Lots of entrepreneurs have two jobs. In fact, some pick up part-time work with benefits because as an entrepreneur you likely won't have any benefits through your business in the early days. There's no shame in working on your dream part-time while you also hold down something steady in the short-term.

You will encounter many disappointments throughout your journey. Know that everyone else experiences the same little hiccups. They are unavoidable. And thankfully, they make you stronger; you learn and grow from the mini-failures.

Before you decide to quit, remember that Rome wasn't built in a day. If the great ancient civilization never continuously advanced architecture and technology, the world we know today would be a much less advanced one. Don't give up and you can maybe even change the world if your idea is big enough.

Be realistic before you decide you want to quit your entrepreneurial endeavour. Give yourself time to make progress. Look at your successes over a span of several months or years so you can see how far you've come; what you've built with your life. Understand: the goals you are trying to achieve are a process not a single event. It takes time. Stick with it.

Don't let setbacks and difficulties discourage you. You'll experience tons of setbacks, just like every other start-up. Learn from them, and then move on. Setbacks and difficulties are your opportunities to become a successful person. You have to lose before you can win.

As an entrepreneur I've made countless mistakes, but I've learned from most of them. People look at me and wonder how I do it, how I overcome one disappointment after another. I've gone through some tough times, but I have faith that has kept me going and prevented me from throwing in the towel.

To expect a perfectly smooth ride to achieve your goal is simply not reasonable. The world doesn't work like that, unfortunately. Why drive yourself crazy expecting perfection? It doesn't exist. Obstacles are the test that will make you feel worthy and proud once you attain your goals. So don't ever quit unless you absolutely have to quit. Be resilient.

3. Business Is Cut Throat. Surround Yourself With Good People

I'll oversimplify here. You will encounter two types of people in business: those who are looking out for your best interest and those who are not. Surround yourself with the former, not the latter. It will take time for you to find and form good alliances, but keep at it through networking. Network all the time, in fact. Do your part, too. Give to others and you'll realize they will reciprocate. Don't always think, "What's in it for me?" If you're honest and helpful, you will attract people who also possess those qualities.

When you find good people, hold on to them. Pay them what they're worth. Treat them with respect. Accommodate their needs. Listen to their ideas. Give them responsibility—you may find that brings out the best in them. Most importantly, once they've proven it time and time again, put trust in good people.

I've worked with so many talented, thoughtful people over the years and I've worked with some who really didn't care at all. I've maintained relationships with those who bring valuable skills and insights to the table. I surround myself with such talents. They inspire me to do better work. They ensure that Single in the City is giving its clientele amazing service.

Owning a business is extremely difficult work. Forget forty hours a week; you'll be pushing eighty or more if you want to make any progress at all in the early stages. Your journey won't be easy. Being an entrepreneur is not as glamorous as it seems. It's endless hours of your time allotted to chasing a dream. You *can* achieve your dream.

Hopefully, I've provided you with advice that will serve as useful throughout your journey toward achieving your entrepreneurial goals. Good luck!!

Laura Bilotta

Laura Bilotta is a dating coach, matchmaker, and the co-founder of successful dating website, *Single in the City dot ca*, which she established in 2002. Since its early beginnings twelve years ago, Laura's efforts and expertise have allowed Single in the City to become one of the largest event-based dating companies in the Greater Toronto Area.

Laura's expert knowledge of dating etiquette, relationships, and human behavior form the basis of her experience. She has hosted over one thousand speed dating/mixer events, coached more than one hundred men and women into becoming dating gurus, and has proudly played matchmaker for countless love-seeking singles.

www.facebook.com/singleinthecity.ca
Twitter: @singleinthecity

Your Life is Your Gift

By Sara Notenboom

For years, I clung tightly to a fairly narrow idea of what constituted success. I subscribed to the notion that success was to be found externally, through the accumulation of achievements and accolades, and the receipt of recognition and approval. I held the idea that I had to prove myself, prove myself worthy, lovable, and ultimately, "normal." I yearned for acceptance, and I wanted more than anything to no longer be seen as different. I carried the idea that if I just achieved enough, people would no longer see me for how I move through the world, but for whom I am beneath the exterior.

I live with a permanent physical disability as a result of acquiring brain damage shortly after I was born. I have Cerebral Palsy, a disorder which typically impacts one's muscle tone, bodily movement and coordination. Fortunately, the way in which it has impacted my body is contained to my legs, meaning that I cannot walk without the use of assistive devices, and that I rely on the use of a wheelchair a majority of the time. Living in a body that appears different from those of most others was in and of itself never a significant issue for me. For this, I am very grateful to my family who never allowed my disability to influence their treatment of me. They made pointed efforts to foster a sense of independence and unlimited capability within me, which had a significant bearing on the development of my self-perception. As such, I have never seen myself as inherently limited or "different." Rather, I have always seen myself as a "normal" person, who simply moves around the world a bit differently. My disability was and is a very small part of my identity. I live with a disability. I am not disabled.

As much as my self-perception is not aligned with associations of weakness, limitation, incapability, helplessness, powerlessness, and so forth, it has been my experience that this is generally not the case in regard to societal perceptions of disability. There have been countless times that I have been placed in something I refer to as the "assumption box" by those with whom I am newly interacting. By "assumption box" I am referring to the pre-conceived notions people carry in regard to those who may fall outside the realm of "normal," and it is this "box" that I spent years trying to get out of by accumulating achievements and chasing recognition. That was, until one of the people from whom I so badly wanted approval told me in a round-about way that I would never receive it from them. As utterly devastating as that was to hear at first, it remains the greatest gift anyone has ever given me. For the first time, I felt truly free. I realized that I had been spending my life chasing that which was not in my control, and that by placing my happiness at the discretion of others I was inadvertently keeping myself powerless, while trying to prove my power.

From that moment on I decided to no longer wait to embrace the life I have been gifted, or to wait on the permission of others to feel good enough. I decided to embrace my imperfections in their fullness, began to redefine my perception of success and decided to make my definition of myself the only one that matters.

When people ask me about my disability, I am always quick to tell them that I am thankful for it, and that I wouldn't change it even if I could. As much as I may have resented the constrictive societal perceptions of disability in the past, I have always known that my disability was given to me for a reason. It has been the catalyst for numerous reflections and insights, and has helped me to come into full realization of my life's purpose. That is, it was only through truly recognizing that I am the only one who holds power over my own life, and who consequently can give me permission to shine unapologetically, that my passion for helping other people come into loving relationships with themselves was fully realized. As such, my motivations for achievement are no longer externally driven. Rather, I am driven by an unrelenting desire to more fully express what I feel I have been put on this planet to do.

I devote my time to spreading a message of unapologetic self-love, and empowering others by getting them in touch with that which is blocking them through counseling, teaching, and writing. I absolutely adore the work that I do, and I wake up each day indescribably grateful that I have the privilege of witnessing the beauty that is the human experience in such an intimate way.

And so, what follows are my tips for success. I invite you to take what resonates and leave the rest.

1. Make it about Expression and Fulfillment.

True success, in my opinion, is all about nurturing our gifts—making our personal evolution our top priority. Honoring ourselves by allowing individual expression to be what we ultimately strive for in all that we do, and in all that we create. It's no longer about "them," and when it's no longer about "them," authenticity shines brightly because we are freed from feeling we need to seek external validation. We can fill ourselves up. Success is about selfish fulfillment; a good and beautiful selfishness that serves to uplift the planet.

When we practice selfish fulfillment, we become happier, gentler, and softer because we recognize that we are here to give of ourselves. That we are, in fact, gifts to the world just by being who we are. We recognize that personal expression is, in and of itself, an act of service. We move away from a mentality of competition and move into a mentality of contribution. It becomes about how much we can give, not about how much we can get. It's about where we are now, not where we're going to be.

2. Recognize the Power of Imperfection

Imperfection, and the necessity of it in our lives, is one of the most profound lessons that living with a disability has taught me. If you were to look for words synonymous with "imperfection" you would most likely find words like defect, deficiency, blemish, fault, weakness, limitation, and so on. Words slanted with negativity that tend to inspire feelings of shame and self-judgment. Words and feelings that foster a sense of disconnection and give strength to the fear that often makes us retreat and become isolated. But here's the thing: Imperfection comes with being human. We all have unique imperfections, visible or invisible. Imperfection is inexorably intertwined with the human experience. Imperfection is universal, shared, and normal, and it is by truly recognizing this that the negativity we often associate with imperfection is dissolved and rendered devoid of its power to keep us small. Instead, imperfection becomes the basis of personal authenticity and connection—it becomes abundantly powerful.

Embracing imperfection frees us. It fosters a sense of gentleness and self-compassion within us that allows us to take chances and to ultimately partake in our own evolution. Consciously embracing our imperfections gives us permission to make mistakes and separate our global sense of worth from any mistakes or failures we may encounter. That is, it allows us to externalize our mistakes and failures and not become wholly defined by them. Instead, mistakes and failures become an expected part of the journey, and they become indications of a willingness to take risks and live fearlessly.

3. Get Comfortable with Fear

Fear is not inherently bad. We need it in order to survive and thrive because without it we would have no way of identifying threat or danger. It protects us—it is needed, normal, and healthy. However, fear becomes problematic when it begins to take on a life beyond our control, when it begins to control each and every decision we make, and thus, prevents us from living life with the zest that we would like to. It can dominate our deepest yearnings by blocking us from fulfilling them, which ultimately truncates the size of our lives and leaves us with perpetual feelings of dis-ease, dissatisfaction, and discomfort.

Here's the thing: discomfort is really the name of the whole game. Discomfort will be present in the act of submitting to our fears as well as in the act of embracing them. It's simply a matter of choice. Discomfort can either function as a mechanism that keeps us small or a mechanism that allows us to push, embrace, and ultimately shine—and that is what fearlessness is. It is the understanding that we can give discomfort the power to foster growth and personal expansion, and that often it can be used to serve us rather than to hinder us.

Your life is your gift, and only you hold the power to decide what you will do with it. Remember that and you will hold the key to success.

Sara Notenboom

Sara Notenboom holds a Bachelor degree in Psychology as well as a Master degree in Counselling Psychology. She works as an individual, couple, and family counsellor, and has a passion for empowering people to live their best life by getting them in touch with what is blocking them—fears, hurts, unhelpful thought patterns, emotional wounds, and so forth. She has worked with countless individuals, and has experience addressing various issues including low self-esteem, grief and loss, anxiety, depression, and trauma. Sara regards her work as her calling and is committed to serving those she works with in a manner that facilitates a sense of safety so she can maximize her clients' capacity for personal growth and change.

Please visit Sara's website at www.saranotenboom.com

Find Your Passion and Keep Tremendously Interested in It—From a Health Coach Who's Been There

By Susana Andres Mignosa

How my passion for fitness and nutrition shapes my life and helps me and others experience the joy of good health and optimal living.

This is my story, how I turned my obsession with exercise and dieting into my passion for fitness and nutrition, and how it shaped my life and now helps me to help others experience the joy of good health and optimal living. This is also a story of how living one's passion tremendously every day can bring one well-being and joy! My passion is fitness and nutrition and I keep tremendously interested in it. From a health coach who has been there, finding that "something" that you are most passionate about and living it tremendously every day brings joy, well-being, and authenticity into one's life.

I'm writing this chapter around the time of year when people often experience a dip with their emotions and energy levels. It's mid-November, pre and post holidays (Thanksgiving and Christmas) and it turns out to typically be a hard time of year for people to feel motivated to exercise and avoid using food as a substitute for the things they are missing or trying to cope with in their lives. Food is so often used by people as a way to pick themselves up from their lows any time of the year, as well. That was certainly the case for me a very long time ago, but I now use food and fitness as a form of positive self-medication. I'm grateful that I eventually learned to use food and exercise for optimal health and happiness and to have discovered ways that I can express my passion and share what I know about healthy eating and fitness with others.

I was always a physically active and athletic child with a healthy appetite for food, competition, and to be the best I could be with my grades and with my sports, be it track and field, basketball, or swimming. Being strong and the best I could be at all I set my mind to do was important to me, but I also wanted to have fun so I didn't put too much pressure on myself. Balance, unknowingly at the time was doing its job—it kept me happy and successful at the same time.

This changed, however, as I became a young adult. I can't quite point out what triggered the onset of my eating disorder. Things changed for me when I was about twenty years old. Rather than lifting weights, running, and eating hearty meals to be strong and healthy, I began to exercise and diet excessively to become thinner like the stereotypical waif models that were in back in the 1990s. I no longer liked my curves or athletic frame. Those were difficult times. I had good relationships with loved ones and friends and one or two not-so-good relationships as well, but I never experienced trauma or abuse or bullying so the cause or causes of what triggered my disorder is something I may never figure out, and that is okay with me now. What I do know is that the skinnier I could get, the better I felt about myself, and the more I liked how I looked because the picture I painted in my head was coming to fruition, and the more in control I felt, as well.

That happiness, however, did not last long, but the struggle with the eating disorder lasted for close to eight years and in time my obsession with my weight and my frail body and lack of self-esteem affected a number of aspects of my life, including my physical and emotional health and the relationships I had with my family and other loved ones. Thankfully, I eventually admitted that I did indeed, have a problem and so I took responsibility for my illness, sought out help, and accepted the help of those who loved me. As I look back, I can see that I had to learn to trust food again and find ways, people, and activities that made me happy because at the time, all I obsessed about was how unhappy I was with myself because of my lack of control with emotional eating and body image. Shame, disgust, and sadness were tough to bear, but in time I began to feel better about myself. I figured out triggers and coping strategies and started to read—a lot—about the psychology of eating disorders and about fitness and nutrition. I also began to exercise again to feel good and strong (not to lose weight) and to cook healthy meals. I began to chew again, slowly, and enjoy the taste of real food again. It was all becoming so holistic! Fitness and food became my medicine to recovering from my eating disorder. It's ironic really, that the same two things that I obsessed about and that made me ill were what was nourishing me with the nutrients, joy, and strength I needed to be healthy.

Things got even better for me when I found out that I was going to be a mother. I was twenty-seven years old, two years into my first marriage, much more in control of my food and weight issues and committed to getting emotionally and physically healthier. I knew then that I couldn't live the way I was living any more (up until then I faced relapses). I had to be healthier, both emotionally and physically, as I was now responsible for the little baby growing inside of me and would soon be her number one source of nourishment, love, safety, and support for the rest of her life. With all the knowledge I received through counselling and self-learning, I began to apply with more intent what I learned throughout my years on the road to recovery, and what I began to re-discover was what I had felt as a young athlete—the holistic benefits of fitness and nutrition. Both gave me so much joy and a sense of well-being, not to mention that I looked better too!

From the time I started to eat healthy, balanced meals during my pregnancy and had joined that blessed prenatal fitness class, to this very day (at the age of forty-one) I have made fitness and nutrition an integral part of my life and that of my family's life.

I began to feel my strongest physically and emotionally in my late thirties. I felt so strongly about how fitness had changed my life that I wanted to share it with others and help them change their lives too. So, I began to share my fitness experiences, health and exercise tips, and healthy recipes through social media and conversations. Then, exactly as they say it happens with the Law of Attraction, I received what I was giving out to the Universe—I was approached and encouraged by the President of Fitness STAR International in Toronto to enter a fitness model competition. Needless to say, my inner voice told to go for it as it was something I used to imagine doing one day when I was a little girl, so I agreed to the challenge and trained hard for three months. I also shared my journey to the Fitness STAR stage with family and friends, both in person and through social media because I felt that it was a good story to motivate others to live their dream or goal. Being accountable was a helpful way for me to stay on track too. People were watching and cheering me on!

The feedback that I began to receive from my daughter, my husband-to-be, my coworkers, friends, and even strangers following me on Facebook and Twitter was extremely positive. That said, it was also unexpected as I was also being thanked many times for inspiring others to lead a healthier life, as well, and was asked for my help and advice. I had created a little ripple effect within my own circle of friends and their friends, and it was very personal to me. I felt so much joy inspiring others, and many times I would feel this personal sense of triumph as well—for that young woman (me) who once felt alone, confused, out of control, ashamed, overweight (when in fact I was extremely underweight) was now developing her optimal physique naturally and inspiring others to get in shape and focus on their goals and dreams too. It was around that time that I knew it was my calling to share my passion for fitness and nutrition with others and to help and encourage others to incorporate fitness and clean eating into their lives for so many different reasons. I knew what I had to do, what I desired to do. In place of becoming a personal trainer (as I had at one time desired to become), I wanted to help others discover the foods and physical activities that would help them achieve optimal health, joy, and well-being. As a health coach and motivational speaker I would be able to share the benefits of integrative holistic nutrition which focusses not only on the food we eat, but also on finding happiness and good health in your relationships, career, physical activity and spirituality.

Back to the competition, I placed fourth out of a stacked seventeen athletic fitness model competitors that August in 2013, and was also given the honor of Audience's Favorite Female Athlete overall. I competed again with Fitness STAR International in March of 2014, and won the title of "1st Place Masters" and brought home two other trophies, as well. I have also published my story with the Fitness STAR Magazine, and I am now a Pro Athlete and Fitness STAR Agency Model. I also have plans to step outside my comfort zone again and compete in another drug-free bodybuilding organization.

I'm now super passionate about optimal living, especially in the areas of fitness and nutrition and in coaching others to live a healthier and happier life. My passion comes from my own personal experience of how fitness and nutrition helped me cope and overcome sad or stressful times during my recovery from an eating disorder, going through a divorce, and other difficult times including the hustle and bustle of every day "stuff." Fitness and discovering healthy foods and recipes is not only a way to stay fit and physically healthy, it has become my natural, self-medicated tool to get over stress, find some alone time for peace and reflection, and to experience the joy one feels from movement and bursts of energy.

This comes from my heart. I use to feel shame and a sense of personal failure for having once had an eating disorder, but I am now at peace with it. In fact, I embrace it and all that I have experienced and learned because of it. I'm on a mission to help others overcome their issues with food, weight, and/or body image, and to encourage physical activity and home-cooked meals as a daily and integral part of everyday living.

If "twenty-something me" could see the present me, she wouldn't believe we are one and the same, but the fact of the matter is that my life now has everything to do with my life then. It is because of "twenty-something me" and what she has gone through that I am who I am today and on this mission of continuous learning, optimal health and coaching others to live a healthier, happier life. The obsession that "twenty-something me" had with food and dieting and exercise has turned into my passion, and I live it tremendously.

My passion for fitness and nutrition continues to shape my life and keep me healthy and full of vitality. I'm a fitness model, motivational speaker, health coach, student of the school of Integrative Nutrition, and I recently created my new website *Rejuvenate Yourself xo* where I blog about a number of things including healthy recipes, exercise tips, and words that motivate us to stay active and eat well.

My journey, both personally and professionally, has taught me a number of things about success in all areas of life, and about the importance of overcoming hardships and challenges in order to live a life of purpose and joy. These are the three nuggets of wisdom that I would like to share with you today:

1. Take responsibility and be grateful for the choices you made (or will have to make) and for the mistakes you made and for your trials and tribulations.

2. Take action to eliminate what doesn't serve you and embrace what does.

3. Keep tremendously interested in that something that you are most passionate about at every stage of your life, every day of your life.

May you take responsibility, always be grateful for your accomplishments and the things you are blessed with, take action, and keep tremendously interested in that something that you are most passionate about, for when you do, you will experience the joy and well-being of living your authentic self and will you inspire others to do the same.

Take it from a health coach who has been "there."

END

Susana's top three favorite quotes about success:

"Have the courage to follow your heart and your intuition. They somehow know what you truly want to become."
—Steve Jobs

"Knowing is not enough, we must apply. Willing is not enough, we must do."
—Bruce Lee

"Find something you're passionate about and keep tremendously interested in it."
—Julia Child (BrainyQuote.com: Julia Child)

Susana Andres Mignosa

Susana Andres Mignosa was born in Toronto, Ontario and raised in Vaughan, Ontario.. She is a mother to an intelligent, strong, confidant, kind girl who is about to turn fourteen years of age. Having raised her daughter as a single mom for close to eleven years, Susana takes pride in that accomplishment for she truly believes in being her young daughter's most influential steward and is consciously focused on leading by example. Both this mindset and responsibility have enabled Susana to work hard and establish herself as a successful business development officer at The Hospital for Sick Children.

Susana is more than a business development officer in health care; she also has a passion that defines who she truly is. She struggled with an eating disorder as a young adult and decided to make a life-altering change after she found out that she was about to become a mother in 2001. Her philosophy was and continues to be that there is always time in a day for exercise and eating a healthy, balanced meal. A few years later, Susana began to take her passion for fitness and weight training to the next level.

Susana's fitness career includes competing professionally as a physique athlete and running marathons. Her accomplishments to date include: Female Audience Favorite overall at the Fitness STAR International World Fitness Model competition in Toronto in August of 2013, first place bikini in the Masters category at the Fitness STAR International in Mississauga, Ontario in March 2014, as well as a number of other exceptional titles. With the fervent desire to help people be the best that they can be, Susana engages people as a motivational speaker, fitness writer, cover model, blogger, and a holistic health coach through her program, *Susana Andres Mignosa, Rejuvenate Yourself xo.*

Susana's commitment to using a holistic and integrative approach to helping her clients take their necessary steps to living a healthier, happier, fitter and more nourishing life is very powerful. She plans to continue making positive ripple effects in the lives of others based on what she knows works and what she knows can make us all happier and healthier.

Please visit Susana at:

http://susanaandres-mignosa.com
htty://susanaandres-mignosa.healthcoach.integrativenutrition.com/health-coaching "

DYNAMO Entrepreneur
Chief Architect of WOW:
James Erdt

LIVING WELL & DOING GOOD

James Erdt is the Visionary and Founder of DYNAMO Entrepreneur, Joyzone Inc. and Fitness STAR International, which are innovative, socially responsible organizations dedicated to guiding people of all ages in fitness, nutrition and inspiration with leading edge products, speaking events and workshops. James has proven perseverance, resourcefulness and vision required to meet the greatest of challenges.

James now shares his story of overcoming addictions, negative environments, spinal surgery and near death situations as a young man with others to support and inspire them on their own life path and evolutionary journey. He is actively involved in philanthropy and chooses to give back on a global scale. Through his practical real world guidance, James shows others how to find the passion, courage, strength and most importantly, the available resources to live out their dreams with purpose while contributing to a better world in the process. His main focus is to guide others to become their best, both personally and professionally in the NOW, so they too can support their own circle of influence and lead by example.

James will support you with valuable tips, tools and some of his best success secrets inspiring joy, abundance and healthy active living.

James Erdt is available for speaking, seminars, workshops & success coaching. For bookings, please contact him directly online at:

DYNAMOentrepreneur.com
or
JamesErdt.com

James Erdt
Speaker, Author & Success Coach

Thank you!
Namaste,